LOOKING BACK AT BRITAIN

TOWARDS A NEW MILLENNIUM

1990s

LOOKING BACK AT BRITAIN

TOWARDS A NEW MILLENNIUM

1990s

Jeremy Harwood

Reader's Digest | gettyimages

CONTENTS

1990s IMAGE GALLERY
FRONT COVER: Skateboarders practise their art with the half-raised London Eye behind them in October 1999.
BACK COVER: The Blairs move in to Downing Street, May 1997.
TITLE PAGE: Members of the public add their contributions to the ever-growing collection of flowers left outside the gates of Kensington Palace following the death of Princess Diana in August 1997.
OPPOSITE: A couple walk down Horse Guards Parade during the annual Gay Pride march in London in 1994.
FOLLOWING PAGES:
A fountain in Trafalgar Square offers relief from the heatwave in August 1997; the 1990s was the hottest decade of the 20th century.
Waiting for a bus in a snowy London town in January 1991.
Members of the audience join the band on stage at a New Age festival in Stoke Newington, London, in 1993.
There was genuine optimism and excitement at Labour's election victory in May 1997; here, press photographers celebrate the new Prime Minister's arrival in Downing Street.

THATCHER'S
DOWNFALL

The decade kicked off with a tempestuous year. In February 1990 freak winds gusting to more than a hundred miles an hour lashed the country, bringing floods and devastation in their wake. As the year continued the country saw poll tax riots and military involvement in the first Gulf War. It ended as it began, with a storm, but this one was political as Margaret Thatcher, leader of the Conservatives since 1975 and Prime Minister since 1979, was driven out of office by an internal rebellion among Tory MPs.

CAN'T PAY, WON'T PAY An effigy of Margaret Thatcher is pilloried during an anti-poll tax demonstration in May 1990. The label, claiming that the premier was the 'real mad cow', is a reference to BSE, a fatal brain disease affecting British cattle.

A QUESTION OF LEADERSHIP

There were good reasons for the Conservative disarray. Although Margaret Thatcher had won three general elections in a row, she was widely unpopular. She had always polarised opinion in the country, but her band of loyal supporters were now dwindling and her hectoring ways had even alienated some leading members of her Cabinet. The Party was dangerously split between pro and anti-Europeans, with the Prime Minister herself heading the latter camp, but it was her decision to impose what she insisted on calling the 'community charge' – known to everyone else as the poll tax – to take the place of the old local government rating system that aroused the most bitter resentment nationwide. No matter how many times Mrs Thatcher assured Britons that the new tax was far better than the old one, people saw it as unfair and divisive.

Fighting off the poll tax

On paper at least, the notion of a community charge seemed fairer than the rating system it was designed to replace. For years, local authorities had been relying largely on some 14 million property owners to provide money to pay for the services they provided (the rents of private tenants normally included an element to cover the rates payable on the property). As the spending of councils increased, the burden on ratepayers proportionately increased. The way around this, Mrs Thatcher and her supporters believed, was to make all those who voted for local councils pay towards their cost. It would mean, she argued, lower bills for many homeowners; it would also make councils more responsive to their voters. The trouble was with the way in which it was decided to implement the reform.

As it emerged, the poll tax was what, technically, is termed a regressive measure. It meant, simply, that the poorest in the land would pay as much as the richest. 'The Poll Tax', one anti-poll tax leaflet claimed, 'will take a uniform sum from each adult living in a particular district. This means that a millionaire living in a mansion will contribute no more than a worker living in a council flat. It means that a family with children aged over 18 living in an overcrowded house will pay more than a rich couple living in a large house.' It continued rhetorically: 'Are we going to let them get away with it?'

'We grabbed carrier bags and filled them with soil, trying to block air vents and stop the water coming in. But it didn't work ...'

Dennis Huxley-Owen, resident of Towyn near Abergele, North Wales

STORM AND FLOOD

The railway line offers the only dry place in sight, and even some of that is underwater, after the coast of North Wales was battered by mountainous seas and gale-force winds in February 1990. The combination of strong winds with an unusually high tide resulted in towering waves that breached a stretch of the defensive sea wall between Towyn and Kinmel Bay, near Abergele. Some 6,000 residents were forced out of their homes and evacuated to safety.

North Wales saw more than its fair share of the stormy weather that affected Britain at the start of 1990 in what was one of the worst winters for storms on record. The storm that hit on 25 January, Burns Day, was the most widespread and destructive. Winds of more than 100mph – Aberporth recorded 108mph – blasted the country during the daytime, killing 47 people.

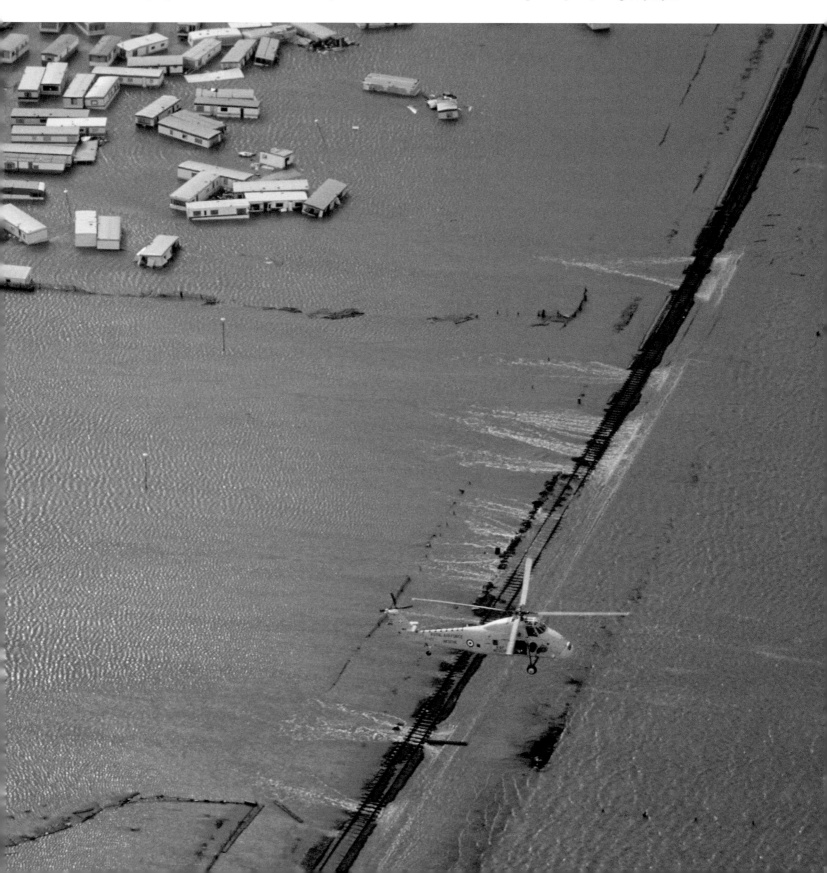

ON THE MARCH
A pensioner puts his point across to a photographer on a mass demonstration protesting against the poll tax – or the 'community charge', as Margaret Thatcher preferred to call it – staged on 31 March, 1990, the day before the hated tax became law in England and Wales. Thousands of demonstrators gathered in London to take part in the protest, which started peacefully enough. Demonstrator Lizzie Woods, then a 16-year-old schoolgirl, recalled: 'There were thousands of ordinary people on the march – families, pensioners, black and white people, and mothers with push chairs. I've never seen so many people who didn't deem themselves political on a march. The mood was really upbeat and the police were happily chatting to people.' Then the mood changed to 'complete chaos in the blink of an eye'. What followed over the next few hours was the worst riot seen in the capital for more than a century. At least 113 demonstrators and many policemen were injured; 400 people were arrested. Other, less violent, demonstrations took place elsewhere around the country.

The people's response was a resounding 'No'. In Scotland, where the tax was implemented first, many refused to fill in the necessary registration forms. Mass-burnings of the hated pieces of paper were organised on convenient local hill-tops. The protests swiftly spread with the aim of making the collection of the tax as expensive, inefficient and unpopular as possible. 'If resistance is widespread and determined enough', a protest pamphlet proclaimed, 'then the State will be forced to keep the rates or at least to alter the poll tax so that it is less punishing than planned.' The poll tax turned into a battle of wills between on the one hand Mrs Thatcher and her supporters in government and on the other much of the nation.

'The lady's not for turning' – again

A battler to her fingertips, Mrs Thatcher seemed to relish the prospect of a fight, but others were not so certain. While whether or not to introduce the tax was being debated in the Cabinet, Nigel Lawson, the Chancellor of the Exchequer, tried to talk the Prime Minister out of it, telling her that it would be 'completely unworkable and politically catastrophic'. He argued in vain. So, too, did rebel Conservative MPs when the legislation came before the House of Commons. They attempted to amend it, dividing the tax into three bands so that it bore some relation to people's ability to pay. They, too, failed. Mrs Thatcher brushed all objections aside. Though she conceded that the tax might have to be capped and that exemptions might have to be considered, she pressed on, determined to introduce it as originally planned.

On 1 April, 1990, the poll tax came into effect nationwide. The day before, an estimated 200,000 demonstrators marched through the streets of central London in protest. They came from virtually every town and city in the country and were joined by thousands of Londoners, who were just as determined to register their opposition to the tax. Outside the capital, 50,000 anti-poll tax demonstrators marched in Glasgow; even in sleepy genteel Hastings, on England's south coast, 10,000 protesters gathered to make their objections heard.

In London, the day of protest began peacefully enough. Steve Eason, a photographer who was taking pictures of the demonstration, recalled: 'It started off as pleasant and good natured. The atmosphere was calm, but near Parliament Square a police officer told me to expect violence.' The unnamed policeman was soon proved right and the proceedings degenerated into a full-scale riot. Branches of Body Shop, Barclays Bank, Tie Rack, Armani and Liberty were among the commercial targets that came under attack. A pall of smoke hung over the streets, which became littered with the overturned remnants of burnt-out cars.

The centre of the disturbance was Trafalgar Square, where a huge crowd of demonstrators found themselves penned into the square by the police. 'Coming back into the square,' Eason remembered, 'the scene looked like the tapestry of the battle of Hastings, with sticks and missiles flying through the air, and police officers in gladiatorial poses. It was such an astonishing scene.' Eason himself did not escape unscathed. Soon afterwards, he received a blow on the back of his head, for which he needed stitches. 'After that, I walked back down Charing Cross Road and people seemed to be looting shop windows and I saw a burnt-out car ... Trafalgar Square was already being hosed down,' he recollected.

There was further trouble in nearby Whitehall, where a small splinter group of demonstrators made a determined though unsuccessful effort to break through the massive security gates protecting Downing Street. The clashes between protesters and police went on late into the night.

SHIELDS AND STONES
Looking more like a foreign riot squad than British bobbies, officers of the Metropolitan Police advance on demonstrators in Trafalgar Square as a traffic cone and other missiles hurtle towards them. The rioting broke out during a demonstration against the poll tax in London on 31 March, 1990. The mood was ugly and the fighting vicious. One mounted officer recalled how, as he and his colleagues followed demonstrators out of the square, 'there was an angry noise. You could sense the tension. A building was on fire and officers on the ground were trying to sort out scuffles, linking arms and looking frightened. It was not a good situation.' The police claimed that the confrontation was sparked off by troublemakers in the crowd. David Meynell, assistant commissioner of the Metropolitan Police in charge on the day, blamed 'the actions of about 3,000 to 3,500 people in minority groups' who launched 'a ferocious and sustained attack' on his men. The later trials of many of those arrested would show the picture was not so clear cut.

'As far as I can make out practically every member of the Cabinet is quietly and unattributably briefing different editors or members of the Lobby about how awful she is..'

Alan Clark, in his *Diaries*, March 1990

In the aftermath, people were quick to apportion blame. In his diary, Alan Clark, a minister in the Department for Defence, pointed the finger at the 'anarchist scum, random drop-outs and trouble-seekers' who had 'infiltrated the march and started beating up the police'. David Waddington, the Home Secretary, told the House of Commons that, in his view, the incidents were down to 'sheer wickedness'. The Prime Minister was quick to concur with such views. Many others were unconvinced. It gradually emerged that the police had been outnumbered and ill-prepared to cope with the size and scale of the protest. Though the initial violence had been provoked by a relatively small number of extremists, what followed was probably just as much down to a failure to police the situation effectively as to the actions of the protesters.

FROM BOOM TO BUST

The government was faltering on other fronts as well. In particular, the economy was in trouble. Stocks and shares were plummeting, the pound was under intense pressure on the foreign exchange markets, imports were reaching record levels and inflation, which the Conservatives claimed to have conquered, was back. It reached a new high of 8.3 per cent in June 1989. Nigel Lawson, the Chancellor of the Exchequer, reacted by raising interest rates higher and higher – the Bank of England's minimum lending rate would reach an eye-watering 15 per cent in October 1990. That same month Lawson suddenly resigned, angered by criticism levelled at his policies by Professor Alan Walters, Mrs Thatcher's own economic adviser. John Major was shunted sideways from the Foreign Office to replace him at the Treasury.

Both Lawson and Major – together with other members of the government – strongly advocated joining Britain's European Union partners in the Exchange Rate Mechanism (ERM), which, they thought, would help to stabilise the fluctuating pound. Mrs Thatcher did not agree. As the economic downturn worsened, the voices of complaint in the country grew increasingly loud. The rise in interest rates was particularly unwelcome, since it struck at the very roots of the property-owning democracy that Mrs Thatcher and her followers were so proud to have fostered. Thanks largely to the policies of Thatcher's administration, the number of people owning their own homes had risen dramatically. And the trend would continue: by the year 2000 more than twice as many homes were owned by their occupants than had been the case back in 1961.

Higher interest rates meant higher mortgage payments, which many people struggled to pay. House prices started to go down rather than up, leaving many property owners trapped by what became notorious as 'negative equity.' Their homes, it transpired, were now not worth as much as the building societies and banks had been only too willing to lend when times were good. Forced repossessions began to rise at an alarming rate.

Other news did nothing to take people's minds off their money woes. The turmoil in Northern Ireland continued, while further afield Iraq's blitzkrieg occupation of Kuwait in August 1990 triggered an international storm of protest.

UNHAPPY RELATIONS
Mrs Thatcher poses with her Cabinet after her government reshuffle in July 1989. Behind the forced smiles, all was not well. Although still sitting at her right hand, Sir Geoffrey Howe had been demoted from Foreign Secretary to Leader of the House of Commons and Deputy Prime Minister. Nigel Lawson (seated on her left) remained Chancellor of the Exchequer, but relations between him and the Prime Minister could by this time be described as frosty. John Major (standing behind Howe) had been promoted to Foreign Secretary; Douglas Hurd (behind Lawson) was Home Secretary. By autumn 1989, Lawson had resigned from the Treasury and been replaced by Major, with Hurd moving to the Foreign Office. One of the few non-smiling faces is that of Chris Patten (front row standing, third from left), who disagreed with Margaret Thatcher on practically everything. Her fall from office would be sparked by the resignation of Geoffrey Howe in November 1990.

Britain was now preparing to take part in a military intervention to expel the invaders as part of a United Nations-backed coalition led by the USA (see page 40).

There were gloomy tidings on the sporting front in England, too. A rejuvenated national football team, under the management of Bobby Robson, had battled its way through the qualifying stages to reach the 1990 World Cup, which was held in Italy that summer. There, England made it to the semi-finals, only to lose 4-3 to West Germany in a penalty shoot-out after the two sides had tied 1-1 after extra time. It was no consolation that the Germans went on to beat Argentina in the final.

Spend, spend and spend

Before the crash the British people, it appeared, had never been better off, though much of this supposed wealth was in fact borrowed. Credit cards were becoming a national addiction; by the end of the decade, half of all adults in the country carried at least one and many had several. They made the hitherto unaffordable instantly affordable as even the poor, it seemed, could now afford a telephone, washing machine and colour television, but many shoppers soon discovered they would pay dearly for the privilege.

The new wealth was by no means distributed equally around the nation. With heavy industries, such as mining and ship-building, in rapid decline, the northeast, Wales, much of Scotland and Northern Ireland were substantially less well off than the southeast and other prosperous regions. Britain was in real danger of becoming two nations, divided into the 'haves' and 'have nots' rather than by social status and class.

The credit boom not only fuelled a sea-change in the way people lived, but also in what they came to expect out of life. As relatively recently as 1951, more than 37 per cent of British households managed without bathrooms or showers; by 1991, less than 1 per cent of homes lacked these basic amenities. The way in which homes were heated was revolutionised as well. In 1964, only around 8 per cent of dwellings enjoyed the luxury of central heating, with 92 per cent relying on coal fires or the gas or electric equivalent; by 2000, these figures had reversed, with 91 per cent of houses having central heating. Home-owners were spending more and more on kitting out their newly bought houses and apartments. Telephones, televisions, refrigerators, freezers and washing machines were considered the first essentials; they were followed by a host of other domestic desirables, such as camcorders, compact disc players, microwaves, personal computers and mobile phones.

PIPPED AT THE POST

Soccer star Paul Gascoigne tries to stem his tears (left) after being yellow-carded – unfairly, as replays would show – in the 1990 World Cup semi-final against West Germany; whatever the result, the booking meant he would miss taking part in the final. In the event, England lost in the penalty shoot-out, with Stuart Pearce and Chris Waddle failing to score. Gascoigne's tears won the hearts of the British public, who voted him BBC Sports Personality of the Year. It was England's best performance in the World Cup since 1966 when they had won the competition, but it was not enough to save the manager Bobby Robson (above). The Football Association did not renew his contract and he left England for a successful career in Europe, managing PSV Eindhoven then Sporting Lisbon, Porto and Barcelona. He was voted European manager of the year in 1996-7.

The shopping revolution

Burgeoning car ownership was another characteristic of the times. Back in 1950, there had been just under two million private cars on Britain's roads. By 2000, there were 23 million cars and people had come to regard them as an essential convenience; 73 per cent of all households enjoyed the regular use of a car.

What this motoring boom led to was a major change in how people lived, particularly when it came to the weekly shop. As the number of cars inexorably increased, traffic congestion built up in town centres throughout the land. Parking was another problem; not only was it becoming increasingly expensive, but also the number of parking spaces available could not keep pace with demand. The solution according to planners and developers was to build huge out-of-town superstores and shopping malls, encouraging people to abandon traditional stores and high streets. By the mid-1990s, the country had 1,102 superstores – in 1973, there had been 43 – and 250 purpose-built shopping malls had been established. Some of the latter were truly enormous. The five largest retail parks, as they were quickly labelled, were Meadowhall outside Sheffield, Merry Hill in Dudley, the MetroCentre at Gateshead, Brent Cross in London and Lakeside near Thurrock. Between them they soon attracted up to 20 million shoppers a year. Even more

massive retail developments were to follow – Cribbs Causeway in Bristol, the
Trafford Centre near Manchester and Bluewater in Kent. With 320 shops and
13,000 car park spaces, Bluewater took the title of largest retail and leisure
complex in Europe.

The changing High Street

Local shops were the big losers. By 1997
Britons were purchasing 76 per cent of
their food at supermarkets, while bakers,
butchers, grocers and greengrocers across
the land were feeling the pinch. Between
1990 and 1995, some 1,500 family
bakeries were forced out of business.
The remaining 3,500 were producing only
8 per cent of the nation's bread.
Traditional village stores were the hardest
hit. According to the Rural Development Commission, the number of food shops
in English villages fell from 9,000 to just under 5,000 between 1991 and 1997 – a
truly astonishing fall of 44 per cent in just six years. It was the beginning of the
end for a way of life that had flourished for centuries. The so-called mini-marts in
local petrol stations plugged some of the gap, but they were a poor substitute.

New shopping habits meant changes in what people ate as well. Ready-
prepared meals and frozen food became the daily fare as the nation seemed to
give up cooking in favour of microwaveable dishes bought from the supermarket.

> 'Once, shopping was a laborious
> task. Now, it's the quintessential
> good day out. Shopping has
> become an event – an event
> that needs to be designed.'
>
> **George Katodrytis, architect**

RETAIL DOWNTURN

Writer Diane Wood Middlebrook chats to a stallholder in the Little Venice fruit market in Paddington, west London (left), in 1991. Individual greengrocers were rapidly becoming an endangered species. A study conducted by Dr Tim Leunig at the London School of Economics showed that in the ten years from 1992 to 2002, listings for greengrocers in *Yellow Pages* business directories declined by 59 per cent; over the same period butchers declined by 40 per cent and hardware retailers by 34 per cent. It seems that shoppers in Britain were prepared to do without personal service and friendly chat in exchange for lower prices, longer opening hours, easy parking and one-stop shopping. Unable to compete with the superstores and out-of-town retail parks springing up across the land, hundreds of small shop-keepers were simply forced out of business.

OPEN ALL HOURS

Some small retailers fared better than others – particularly if they were willing to put in the hours and stay open late. Here, an Indian family poses for the camera outside their shop on the Camberwell Road in south London. From the mid-1980s onwards, more and more British-Asians switched to self-employment, in particular taking on small corner shops selling groceries, sweets and newspapers. They prospered. By the mid-1990s British Sikhs, in particular, were well on the way to being middle class. Many encouraged their children to be upwardly mobile. By 1995, in the 18 to 27-year-old bracket, Britons of Indian heritage were twice as likely to go to university as whites, seeing a university education as an important stepping stone to a profession. Medicine, the law and engineering were particularly favoured.

TWO NATIONS

In 1987 Margaret Thatcher had famously said that there was 'no such thing as society'. Rather, she continued, 'people must look to themselves' and not rely on the state for support and sustenance. The social and economic policies she pursued were in line with this belief. Many critics felt that what she was promoting would serve only to widen the already increasing gap between the rich and the poor. The wealth divide between north and south was clearly evident in factors such as house prices. Decaying northern cities found themselves starved of the government funds necessary for sustained urban renewal and redevelopment. Scenes of urban decay – like this example in Liverpool (above), once one of the most prosperous conurbations in the land – became all too common. Redevelopment was in evidence at Canary Wharf in London's Docklands (left), but initially at least the gleaming towers and office blocks would bring jobs and prosperity to workers from outside the area, rather than the local East End community.

They were cheap, convenient – slipped into a microwave oven they were ready in minutes – and made a change from the other growing stand-in for real food: the takeaway. Ironically, in this age of prosperity, many people were eating less fresh produce than in the days of rationing during the Second World War. The downside to come would be rising levels of obesity and associated health problems.

The nation's love affair with Indian food continued. By 1997, sales of Indian ready-made meals and snacks were worth a staggering £331 million. Indian restaurants boomed as well; in 1995, there were about 10,000 of them employing 60,000 to 70,000 people with a turnover of £1.5 billion a year – more than the shipbuilding, coal and steel industries combined. It was clear evidence if any were still needed that the traditional industries, for so long the country's economic backbone, were fast approaching terminal decline.

The Channel Tunnel

It was not quite all gloom and doom. Some 30 metres below the seabed of the English Channel, one of the greatest construction projects of all time was well underway. Finally, after decades of prevarication, the Channel Tunnel was to link Britain physically with France and the rest of Europe.

There had been various suggestions as to the best way of accomplishing this daunting task. One was for the construction of a massive suspension bridge – it

continued on page 32

THE CHANNEL TUNNEL

The Channel Tunnel is not one tunnel, but three – one for trains from Britain to France, another for trains running the other way, plus a service tunnel between them. Drilling teams operated from both sides of the Channel and met up under the sea. The project went way over budget but was successfully completed in 1994, when it opened offering passenger train services plus drive-on car and lorry shuttles. In 1996 the American Society of Civil Engineers included the tunnel on their list of the 'Seven Wonders of the Modern World'.

DRILLING A WAY TO FRANCE
The giant Marine Tunnel (South) Boring Machine is readied for action as the Channel Tunnel inches its way towards France. The idea of tunnelling under the English Channel goes back a long way. French mining engineer Albert Mathieu put forward the first design in 1802. A serious attempt was made by private rail developers in the early 1880s, even going so far as digging trial tunnels, but the British government, fearing invasion, put a stop to further development. Another serious suggestion came shortly after Britain joined the EU in 1973, but it was abandoned in 1975 as Harold Wilson's government sought to cut back on expenditure. Finally, in 1984, the British and French governments agreed on the construction of a fixed link between the two countries. Once the decision had been taken, plans were finalised for two single-track rail tunnels with links to a service tunnel between them. Work got underway in 1987 and the end result is the world's second-longest tunnel at 50.5km (31 miles), which contains the longest undersea stretch at 38km (24 miles). The depth of the tunnels varies, reaching a maximum of 75m but averaging 40–45m below the seabed – it was vital that the tunnels were kept within the solid chalk layer beneath the Straits of Dover. At the height of construction, some 13,000 people were employed in the actual tunnelling deep underground. One of the boring machine cutters can be seen on display in Coquelles, the town nearest to the tunnel in France, erected as a monument to the men who worked on the tunnel, ten of whom – eight of them British – died during construction.

BREAKING THROUGH

History was made on 1 December, 1990, when British and French construction workers drilled through the final wall of rock to join the two halves of the service tunnel, the first of the three tunnels that would form the Channel Tunnel link between Britain and France. This photograph (above) was taken as part of the celebrations to mark the occasion and includes the two men – British tunneller Graham Fagg and his French counterpart Philippe Cozette – who made the historic breakthrough. Before assembling to cheer for the camera, the construction team had started with champagne underground, the first time alcohol had been allowed on site, then made their way to the French end of the tunnel where the British contingent had their passports stamped in commemoration. 'The construction team had done brilliantly,' *Contract Journal* editor Andrew Pring reported. 'To drill so precisely from both ends and meet exactly where they had planned to years before was impressive and exciting.' Mrs Thatcher hailed the achievement as a 'tribute to private enterprise'.

The main rail tunnels linked up the following year. The breakthrough moment on the first of these was recorded in this photograph (right), showing British engineers greeting a

'I stood watching Graham Fagg drilling the last few inches of rock that separated us from the French engineers and was able to shake hands through the gap that had opened up. I … recall thinking what a wonderful moment in history it was.'

Andrew Pring, editor with *Contract Journal*, on the breakthrough moment in December 1990

French worker as he climbs through to the British half of the tunnel on 22 May, 1991.

The total bill for construction came in at around £12 billion – almost twice the original budget – but it was an amazing engineering achievement. The tunnel was officially opened by the Queen and President Mitterrand on 6 May, 1994.

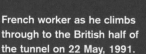

was dubbed *Europont* – rising high above the Straits of Dover to carry road and rail traffic across the Channel, while leaving space for the busy shipping traffic to pass underneath. The proposal was dismissed as too expensive and because the technology required to build it was new and untested. Other schemes called for the construction of road as well as rail tunnels. In the end, the decision-makers opted for a purely rail proposal, combining passenger services between rail terminals in London, Paris and Brussels, with a roll-on roll-off shuttle service carrying cars and lorries from new purpose-built terminals on either side of the Channel.

MRS THATCHER FALLS

By the time the first of the three undersea tunnels had been bored, Britain was under new political management. In December 1990, the same month that British and French engineers met up somewhere under the Channel, the seemingly invincible, unstoppable Margaret Thatcher was forced out of power.

The fall had been a long time coming. Throughout 1990, the pressures on the Prime Minister and her government continually increased. The worsening state of the economy and the consequent rise in unemployment had backbench Conservative MPs running scared. And the party was bitterly divided over its attitude to Europe. Mrs Thatcher did not start her premiership as a Eurosceptic, but she had always opposed any attempt by the European Commission to increase its powers. As her attitude towards the Community became more antagonistic, this led to the events that would bring her down. Two years previously, the Prime Minister had addressed a European summit meeting at Bruges in Belgium on the evils of federalism. Despite efforts by the Foreign Office to get her to tone down her speech, she made her position crystal clear. She had not 'rolled back the frontiers of the state in Britain only to see them reimposed at a European level, with a European super-state exercising a new level of dominance from Brussels.'

Her message was unequivocal and it deeply upset Sir Geoffrey Howe, the luckless Foreign Secretary, who struggled on, hoping to temper the Prime Minister's attitude. Along with Nigel Lawson, he went as far as to threaten to resign if Mrs Thatcher persisted in her opposition to Britain entering the European Exchange Rate Mechanism. She gave way, sulkily, only to strike back in a Cabinet reshuffle by demoting Howe to Leader of the House of Commons. He was also given the title of Deputy Prime Minister, though Bernard Ingham, Mrs Thatcher's press secretary, made it clear to journalists that the position was largely honorific. Howe gritted his teeth and soldiered on.

> '**I have done what I believe to be right for my party and for my country. The time has come for others to consider their own response to the tragic conflict of loyalties with which I myself have wrestled for perhaps too long.**'
>
> **Sir Geoffrey Howe, concluding his resignation speech, 13 November, 1990**

Howe resigns

The last remaining member of Mrs Thatcher's original 1979 Cabinet, Geoffrey Howe had served his leader faithfully for more than 11 years. He seemed the most unlikely person to trigger the final crisis. But now he had had enough. Citing as his reason the Prime Minister's policies towards Europe – in particular, her opposition to the notion of a single European currency – he resigned and retired to the Conservative backbenches. Howe delivered his resignation speech to a packed House of Commons on 13 November, 1990. Every word was political dynamite.

Up to this point, Howe had never been regarded as an inspiring speaker. Denis Healey, the pugnacious Labour ex-Chancellor, had once remarked that being attacked by him was 'like being savaged by a dead sheep'. This time, it was different. Though Howe did not once raise his voice, the House of Commons hung on his every word as he denounced Mrs Thatcher's diplomatic style. Alan Clark recorded the scene in his diary. 'From the moment he rose to his feet, Geoffrey got into it. He was personally wounding – to a far greater extent than mere political differences would justify … The Labour benches loved it. Grinning from ear to ear, they "Oooh'd" and "Aaah'd" dead on cue.'

The Conservatives, in contrast, listened in stunned silence. The television cameras, only recently allowed into the chamber, focused remorselessly on the white-faced Prime Minister sitting on the front bench. Behind Howe, Nigel Lawson could be seen nodding vigorously in agreement with every word. In the face of Mrs Thatcher's 'perceived attitude towards Europe', Howe said, conducting negotiations with the country's Community partners was 'rather like sending your opening batsmen to the crease only for them to find, the moment the first balls are bowled, that their bats have been broken before the game by the team captain.'

Thatcher versus Heseltine

According to Alan Clark, 'Afterwards, a lot of people, semi-traumatised, didn't want to talk about it.' Not so Michael Heseltine, who was ready to do far more than talk. Long regarded by some as the Conservative leader in waiting, he announced the very next day his decision to stand against Mrs Thatcher in the annual leadership contest the party rules decreed had to be held later that month.

THE WOULD-BE KING
Former Cabinet minister Michael Heseltine had frequently declared that he 'could think of no circumstance in which I would challenge Margaret Thatcher'. But that was before Geoffrey Howe resigned from the Cabinet, dealing Mrs Thatcher a serious blow in his resignation speech. It then became clear that Heseltine had simply been waiting for the opportunity to strike. Here he is seen leaving the House of Commons, surrounded by the press and photographers, on 19 November, 1990, a few days after announcing his candidacy for the leadership of the Conservative Party.

'I don't think she realises what a jam she's in.'

Alan Clark, in his diary

The rules of the Tory leadership contest were clear. Mrs Thatcher not only had to win a clear majority of the votes, but she also had to be 15 per cent ahead of her rival in terms of the number of votes cast. She herself was supremely confident of victory. She went to attend a European summit meeting in Paris, leaving it to her acolytes to mobilise her vote. 'The whole house [House of Commons]', Alan Clark recorded, 'is in ferment. Little groups, conclaves everywhere … In the corridors, it is all furtive whispering and glancing over shoulders.' He concluded that a Heseltine bandwagon was rapidly gaining speed. There was not 'a single person working for her who cuts any ice at all.'

ABSENTEE PREMIER
The personal chemistry is clear as Margaret Thatcher meets Mikhail Gorbachev, president of the Soviet Union, on the steps of the British Embassy in Paris in November 1990 (left). The Prime Minister was so confident of victory over Michael Heseltine in the contest for the leadership of the Conservative Party that she stuck to her international schedule, attending the Conference on Security and Cooperation in Europe in the French capital. Her closest supporters were aghast at her decision – they felt she should stay in London to bolster her support – but she refused even to consider returning from Paris for the count. Alan Clark, minister in charge of defence procurement, described it in his diary as 'absolute madness … It just makes her seem snooty and remote'.

The fears of Mrs Thatcher's supporters were justified. After failing to achieve the requisite number of votes to be re-elected on the first ballot, her Cabinet colleagues queued up to tell her that she would not win in the second round. After sleeping on it to consider her position, she decided to resign, reputedly on the advice of her husband Denis. She is seen here (top right) leaving Downing Street for Buckingham Palace on 22 November, 1990, to inform the Queen of her decision to step down as premier once the Conservative Party had elected a new leader. 'We're leaving Downing Street for the last time after eleven-and-a-half wonderful years,' she told reporters when she formally resigned, 'and we're happy to leave the UK in a very much better state than when we came here.'

HOW ABOUT ME?
Once Mrs Thatcher had decided to resign, the field was open to others who would not have considered standing against her. Foreign Secretary Douglas Hurd and John Major, the Chancellor of the Exchequer, both decided to enter the contest against Heseltine. Hurd is seen here (right, seated) with some of his supporters standing behind him. From left to right, they are: Chris Patten, William Waldegrave, John Wakeham, Virginia Bottomley, Tom King, Tim Yeo and Kenneth Clarke.

When the ballot took place on 20 November, Mrs Thatcher won 204 votes against Michael Heseltine's 152 with 16 MPs abstaining. On the face of it, it seems a clear win, but she was four votes short of the magic number she needed for outright victory. Still in Paris, she immediately announced her intention of standing again. 'I fight', she told the BBC, 'and I fight to win!'

Back in London, however, things were not going her way. Far from increasing her vote, as some of her supporters had confidently predicted, the opposite was happening. Slowly but surely, her support was dribbling away. In an attempt to stop the rot, the Prime Minister saw each member of her Cabinet in turn. They did not bring her good news. Douglas Hurd and John Major had agreed to nominate her for the next round of voting, but the message from her other ministers was mixed to say the least. Though most of them said that they would back her if she fought on, they warned her that the probability was she would lose. Only Cecil Parkinson and Michael Portillo offered her unqualified support.

The next morning, Margaret Thatcher announced her resignation as Prime Minister. After a final barnstorming performance in the House of Commons, she drove to Buckingham Palace to tell the Queen of her decision. She would go, she said, as soon as the Conservative Party had elected a new leader. The era of the 'Iron Lady' was over. In the event, her reign had come to an end at a truly breathtaking speed.

GOING, GOING, GONE
A jubilant lady rings a town-crier's bell in celebration as the news of Mrs Thatcher's resignation breaks. The Prime Minister had totally failed to appreciate the upsurge of popular feeling against her – even when opinion polls were showing the Conservatives trailing 28 points behind the Labour opposition. The voters had made their feelings clear in by-election after by-election. In March 1990, Labour overturned a massive Conservative majority of 14,000 in mid-Stafford, while in October the Liberal Democrats captured true-blue Eastbourne from the Tories. Ian Gow, the previous MP for Eastbourne, had been killed that July by an IRA bomb planted under his car, but even the tragic circumstances of his predecessor's death could not help the new candidate to retain the seat for the Conservatives.

The anti-Tory section of the British public, like this lady, enjoyed a cheer when Margaret Thatcher left office, but they would have to wait a few years longer to get rid of the rest. Despite the opinion polls and by-election results, John Major would prove surprisingly resilient when the next general election came around.

THE BOY FROM BRIXTON
John Major, with his wife Norma, waves to the crowd as he enters Downing Street for the first time as Prime Minister. Although Major looks at ease, Norma looks rather startled to find herself about to enter No.10 as the Prime Minister's wife. Major told the waiting reporters that he wanted to 'build a country that is at ease with itself, a country that is confident, and a country that is prepared and willing to make the changes necessary to provide a better quality of life for all our citizens.'

ENTER JOHN MAJOR

After years in the political wilderness – he had resigned from Mrs Thatcher's Cabinet back in 1986 – Michael Heseltine had succeeded in toppling his arch-enemy. But he was not to succeed her as party leader. He had made too many powerful enemies of his own for that. Though he might be the grassroots darling of his party, many Tory MPs regarded him as nothing more than a terminally disloyal political opportunist.

Alan Clark confided to his diary what he thought was the general feeling among Conservative MPs. 'Not so many in the party really want to vote for Heseltine himself. The bulk of Michael's support comes from his so-called election-winning powers. People have guilt about condoning what he did to Her. Once they have a real reason to do so, they'll abandon him.' And as it turned out, Clark's hunch was right.

In the second leadership ballot, Heseltine found himself challenged by John Major and Douglas Hurd, respectively the Chancellor of the Exchequer and Foreign Secretary. No two candidates could have been more dissimilar. Hurd was an old Etonian, who had started off his career as a diplomat before becoming a politician. Rightly or wrongly, he was viewed as a traditional Tory of the old school, who lacked the common touch. Major, by contrast, was a relative newcomer. He had entered Parliament in 1979, in the election that swept Mrs Thatcher to power, and his entire career as an MP had been under her reign. He had enjoyed a meteoric rise to political prominence and power as Thatcher rattled through potential

Cabinet talent in government re-shuffles. His appointment as Chancellor had come after Nigel Lawson's resignation. Major was also by far the youngest of the three leadership candidates.

When the votes were counted on 27 November, Major had garnered 185 supporters to Heseltine's 131 and Hurd's 56. Though his total was still two votes short of the majority required by the rules, it was clear that Major was the winner. Later that evening, Michael Heseltine finally conceded defeat. The following morning, Major was summoned to Buckingham Palace and asked to form a new government.

A nation 'at ease with itself'

The lad from a humble background – after his father's business began to decline, he had been brought up in a small house in Brixton – had made it to the top of the greasy pole. At 47, he was Britain's youngest Prime Minister since Lord Rosebery, almost a century before. In outlining his political credo, Major talked of building a 'society of opportunity' and making privileges that had been the preserve of 'the few' available 'to the many.' After the up-and-down switchback ride of the Thatcher years, this seemed to be what people were looking for. In Alan Clark's words 'people are sick of passion, they want reassurance', and that was exactly what Major appeared to be offering.

In his public manner at least, Major reminded people of a friendly neighbour, the affable character with a winning smile who might well be the man next door. He was calm, good humoured, seemingly imperturbable, self-deprecating and, above all, likeable and decent. He seem totally lacking in pretension. Moreover, though Mrs Thatcher might claim the credit for his emergence – she would, she promised (or warned), be a good 'backseat driver' – he was determined to demonstrate that he was his own man. He, not she, would make the decisions and policies that would put the country back on a path towards easier times.

It was not going to be an easy task. The poll tax still hung like a millstone around the government's neck. Michael Heseltine, now back in the Cabinet as Secretary of State for the Environment, was given the urgent task of coming up with a viable substitute for it. There was an imminent war to be fought in the Gulf. The continued weakness of the economy had to be tackled. And there was the ever-present threat posed by the IRA.

On 8 February, 1991, Major had direct experience of how real that threat was. Three mortar shells, triggered by remote control from an abandoned van, were fired at 10 Downing Street. One exploded in the backyard, rattling the bulletproof glass in the windows of the Cabinet room, where Major was presiding over a meeting of his War Cabinet. 'I think we'd better start again somewhere else', he calmly said to his colleagues. No major structural damage was done; three people were slightly wounded. The intention was obvious, as Major immediately recognised. 'I think it was clear', he told the House of Commons that afternoon, 'that it was a deliberate attempt this morning both to kill the Cabinet and to damage our democratic system of government.'

Above all, though, there was the question of Britain's relationship with the European Community, which had brought about Mrs Thatcher's downfall. Would 'nice Mr Major', as people were quick to label him, be able to keep the Tory Eurosceptics in check and hold his bitterly divided party together, while at the same time successfully resisting the demands of the bureaucrats in Brussels?

LABOUR ON THE UP
Neil Kinnock and above him on the steps a young Peter Mandelson, then the party's Director of Communications, on their way to a Labour Party meeting in Clapham, south London, in July 1990. Kinnock had been elected to the party leadership as successor to Michael Foot following Labour's crushing general election defeat in 1983. Kinnock's mission was to rebuild his demoralised party and over the years he fought to make Labour electable, cracking down on militant left-wingers within the party ranks and modernising the old-fashioned party machine. He had failed to oust Margaret Thatcher in 1987, but did at least significantly reduce her majority. By the time of the next general election Conservative MPs had ousted her themselves, and perhaps Kinnock took heart in facing the mild-mannered John Major rather than the Iron Lady herself. As Labour's campaign built towards the 1992 election, Kinnock had every reason to be confident of victory. He was to be sorely disappointed.

THE FIRST GULF WAR

British engineers from the 7th Armoured Brigade blow up a minefield shielding Iraqi positions in the Saudi Arabian desert (right). A woman stands among crosses and mock gravestones during a mass demonstration outside Parliament against going to war in the Gulf (below). A bloody eight-year war between Iraq and Iran had been over for less than two years when Saddam Hussein ordered Iraqi troops into action once more, this time against Kuwait. Their invasion began on 2 August, 1990, and was complete in three days. Saddam declared Kuwait to be Iraq's 19th province. Perhaps it was the support of Western governments during his war against Iran that persuaded Saddam this move would go unchallenged. If so, he was wrong. The UN Security Council called for immediate, unconditional withdrawal. When the Iraqis refused, the UN authorised military intervention.

In all, 29 countries committed troops to the war that would force Iraq out of Kuwait. The USA took the lead, followed by Saudi Arabia, the UK, Egypt, France, Syria and Morocco. By 15 January, 1991 – the day the final UN ultimatum to Iraq expired – there were 580,000 Allied troops mustered in the Gulf against 540,000 Iraqis. The stage was set for Operation *Desert Storm*. US General Norman Schwarzkopf, who had overall military command, had spent the previous months planning the operation with his staff. It started with massive air attacks both on Iraqi positions in Kuwait and on Iraq itself. So-called smart bombs and cruise missiles rained down on the capital, Baghdad. Then the Allied forces on the ground rolled triumphantly forward. On 27 February, Kuwait City was liberated. US President George Bush ordered a ceasefire to come into effect the following day.

The Iraqis had been routed. More than half the divisions fielded by Saddam Hussein had been destroyed and almost 500,000 Iraqi soldiers taken prisoner. The dictator had lost what he had vaingloriously called 'the mother of all battles'. It was, said one US soldier in the 4th Armoured Division, 'a great turkey shoot'. General Sir Peter de la Billiere, the senior British commander, said 'I could have had my tanks in Baghdad within 24 hours'. Captain Sebastian Willis Fleming, in command of a unit of British soldiers advancing up the Basra road, was less sanguine. 'Funnily enough', he recalled, 'the thing I found most distressing, I would say, was the smell of cheap perfume.'

ANNUS
HORRIBILIS

It was, said the Queen in a speech given at London's Guildhall in November 1992, 'not a year on which I shall look back with undiluted pleasure'. In the 40th anniversary year of her accession to the throne, she had watched helplessly as the marriages of her children fell apart. Princess Anne divorced Captain Mark Phillips. The Duke and Duchess of York announced their separation. Most public of all, the fairytale wedding of the Prince and Princess of Wales came to a very bitter end. And as if to show that things can always get worse, the Queen's 'annus horribilis', to use her phrase, rounded off with a disastrous fire at Windsor Castle. Things went badly wrong for others, too, among them Labour leader Neil Kinnock and the new Chancellor of the Exchequer, Norman Lamont. Perhaps it was all in the stars.

LONE PRINCESS The Princess of Wales poses alone outside the Taj Mahal in Agra during the royal couple's state visit to India in 1992. Her marriage to the Prince of Wales was obviously on the rocks.

A BUMPY RIDE

Taking over from Margaret Thatcher as Prime Minister was never going to be easy for John Major. Conservative MPs and non-Tories up and down the land might have been happy that she had gone, but the grassroots Tory Party were appalled by what had happened. Nevertheless, Major got off to a good enough start.

His first big challenge as Prime Minister was the Gulf War, which was quickly over as the UN's international coalition force made short work of liberating Kuwait from Iraqi occupation. For British troops taking part, their allies proved almost as dangerous as the Iraqi forces ranged against them: an accidental American hit – an incident of so-called 'friendly fire' – on a Warrior armoured vehicle killed nine British soldiers. The total British death toll was 24.

Backtracking on the poll tax

On the home front Major quickly declared his intention of dealing with the detested poll tax. Michael Heseltine, the newly appointed Environment Secretary in Major's Cabinet, was given the job of devising a substitute for Thatcher's 'community charge'. In the meantime, in the hope of lessening the widespread resentment at paying the tax, Chancellor Norman Lamont announced a reduction in the poll tax payable by individuals of £140, to be paid for by a rise in the rate of VAT. In the case of one borough, Conservative controlled Wandsworth in south London, this had the effect of reducing its community charge to zero.

The proposal that Heseltine eventually came up with was the council tax, which came into effect in 1993 and was generally perceived to be much fairer than the poll tax. It also bore a remarkable resemblance to the old system of rates that had just been abolished. Although most of the nation rejoiced, Mrs Thatcher resented the decision to abandon the poll tax and soon turned from a John Major fan – after her resignation she had backed his candidacy for the leadership – into a critic. She was not alone. Newspapers were quick to savage Major for 'dithering' as he struggled to get a grip. The *Daily Mail* unforgivingly dismissed his government as 'pathetic', the *Financial Times* said it was 'exhausted' and the *Daily Telegraph* complained that it lacked any 'sense of direction'.

Opinion polls and by-elections all told a similar story. In March 1991 the Liberal Democrats trounced the Conservatives in the Ribble Valley, capturing a safe Tory seat on a 25 per cent swing away from the government. Two months later the Tories lost 900 seats in the local elections and in another by-election at Monmouth Labour took the seat

FREE AT LAST
One piece of very good news that came in John Major's first year in power was the freeing of British journalist John McCarthy after more than five years in captivity in Lebanon. Here, McCarthy waves to well-wishers as he steps out of an RAF transport plane at Lyneham military airbase on 8 August, 1991. His father Pat stands beside him. McCarthy had been kidnapped in Beirut by Islamic Jihad guerrillas in April 1986 and held hostage by them ever since. Jill Morrell, his girlfriend at the time who led the campaign to press for his release, was 'ecstatic' that at long last he had regained his freedom. 'There were times', she said, 'when it seemed like it would take forever and times when it seemed like it had been going on for an eternity.' McCarthy expressed particular gratitude to his fellow hostages – Brian Keenan, released the previous year, and Americans Terry Anderson and Tom Sutherland and fellow-Briton Terry Waite who were still held captive – for their morale-boosting support during the ordeal. Terry Waite was released in November 1991.

'The Bill will abolish the poll tax and replace it with the council tax. The council tax is a fair and straightforward method of raising local government revenue … based on the market value.'

Michael Heseltine announcing the Local Government Finance Bill to Parliament, November 1991

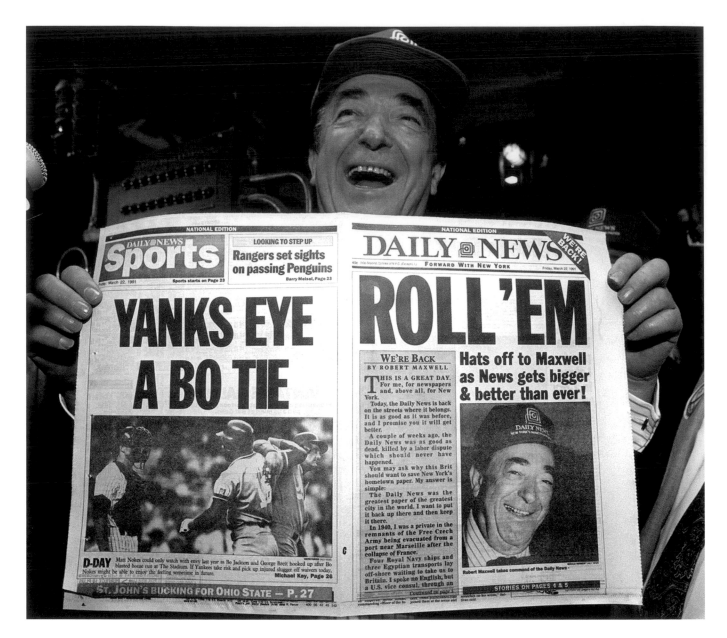

from the Conservatives with a swing of 13 per cent. It could be argued that such
results would have been expected even with Thatcher still in office, but it still
seemed evident to many that, when the next general election came, Neil Kinnock
and Labour would sweep to power.

The Maxwell scandal

Perhaps Major was just plain unlucky
with the timing of events. When
swashbuckling, larger-than-life media
tycoon Robert Maxwell met his
mysterious death – he vanished
overboard from the *Lady Ghislaine*, his luxury private yacht, and drowned off the
Canary Islands in November 1991 – the Prime Minister was quick to join in the
public tributes. This remained in people's minds when it soon became clear that
the dead multi-millionaire had committed fraud on a truly epic scale.

'Mirror, Mirror on the Wall, Who is the Biggest Crook of All'

Sun headline as details of the Maxwell scandal emerged

BOUNCING CZECH

Never shy of blowing his own trumpet, beaming media mogul Robert Maxwell celebrates his first edition of the *New York Daily News* in March 1991, with himself as the front-page story. By this time, Maxwell was deep in financial trouble, with debts of around £2 billion. Then, in November 1991, he drowned off the Canary Islands, having gone missing from his yacht, the *Lady Ghislaine*. The circumstances of his death remain mysterious – there were rumours of links to MI6 and with Mossad, the Israeli secret service, prompting conspiracy theorists to suspect murder. Given the appalling state of his business affairs, others believe it was suicide to avoid going to jail. The official verdict was accidental drowning. In the aftermath of his death it emerged that Robert Maxwell had ruthlessly plundered the pension funds of his workers in the two public companies under his control, stealing hundreds of millions of pounds from them. His much vaunted wealth, it transpired, was more illusion than reality and his bloated business empire collapsed like a pricked balloon. Two of his sons – Kevin and Ian Maxwell – struggled to keep the sinking ship afloat, but they were forced to file for bankrupty in 1992. With debts of £400 million, Kevin became Britain's biggest bankrupt. Both brothers faced investigation by the Fraud Squad.

SINS OF THE FATHER

Kevin Maxwell leaves the Old Bailey in 1996 after being found not guilty of fraud. His brother Ian and his father's former financial adviser, Larry Trachtenberg, were also acquitted of fraudulent misuse of pension fund assets stolen by Robert Maxwell. Ossie Fletcher, one-time editor of the Maxwell-owned *Sporting Life*, commented 'we always assumed that the pension fund was untouchable'. But the unscrupulous Robert Maxwell had boasted that 'I own the pension fund'. The trial had lasted eight months and cost some £25 million; it took the jury 48 hours and 17 minutes to come to their unanimous not-guilty verdicts.

Desperate to raise cash to shore up his crumbling media empire, which had run up debts well in excess of £2 billion, Robert Maxwell resorted to stealing hundreds of millions of pounds from his employees' pension funds. He then used this money to buy back his own shares in an attempt to boost the share price and so keep his leaky enterprises afloat. He also pledged the same stocks several times over as collateral for some of his many loans. Though his sons Ian and Kevin desperately tried to stave off the inevitable following their father's death, the crash – and bankruptcy – followed. The 'Man Who Saved The Mirror', as the *Daily Mirror* had headlined its tribute to its dead proprietor, was unmasked as the biggest fraudster of the century.

The two Maxwell brothers were arrested and charged with being active accomplices to their father in the fraud, though they were eventually cleared. In the meantime, as the legal proceedings rumbled on, a House of Commons Select Committee chaired by Labour MP Frank Field called for root-and-branch reform of the pension law to prevent anything remotely like Maxwell's thefts from happening again. Field and his fellow backbenchers blamed City of London watchdogs, Maxwell's own bankers, the auditors of his accounts and a host of other financial advisers for failing to detect and blow the whistle on his appalling business irregularities. Referring to the great and the good who were summoned to testify, the select committee commented scathingly: 'Pontius Pilate would have blushed at the spectacle of so many witnesses washing their hands in public of their responsibilities in this affair.'

Many outside Parliament thought the stable door was being shut after the horse had well and truly bolted. Ivy Needham, a 67-year-old partially-sighted widow from Leeds who was one of Maxwell's many victims, commented that 'pensions were supposed to be gilt-edged security'. It certainly looked as though white-collar crime paid.

MAJOR FINDS HIS FEET

It was a combination of circumstances that started to turn the tide in Major's favour. The economy slowly began to improve. Interest rates were lowered as inflation fell back to 4 per cent. Above all, there was the Prime Minister's successful conclusion of the Maastricht Treaty with Britain's Continental partners, which turned the Common Market into the European Union.

Mastering Maastricht

There were those who hailed Maastricht as a triumph for Major. *The Times*, for instance, declared that it was 'game, set and match to Britain'. Others were not so sure. Though Major managed to paper over the divisions within his own party, the Eurosceptic MPs were far from content. They believed that in agreeing to the treaty Major had, in principle, consented to work towards a European super-state at some point in the future. To judge by some interpretations of the agreement, they were not far off the mark. German Chancellor Helmut Kohl said that 'within a few years [the treaty] will lead to the creation of what the founding fathers of modern Europe dreamed of after the war, the United States of Europe'. For his part, Major pledged that Britain lay firmly 'at the heart of Europe'. Such words were anathema to the Eurosceptics, Mrs Thatcher being prominent among them.

Nevertheless, there was no doubt that, through patient negotiation, Major had extracted significant concessions at Maastricht, and he gained respect as a result. He had won the right for Britain to opt out of any future monetary union and also to disregard the provisions of the treaty's so-called social chapter, including the introduction of a compulsory minimum wage.

Unexpected victory

Buoyed up by his triumph, Major decided the time had come to go to the country. After Norman Lamont set out a tax-cutting budget, Major announced the very next day that the general election would be held on 9 April, 1992. Most predicted a Labour victory or a hung parliament, but it soon turned into a much tighter and hard-fought contest.

After a slow start, the Prime Minister found his campaigning feet. Standing on a traditional soap box, he put his case directly to the man on the street. It was a refreshing approach. Tory tactics made the most of Major's humble origins and warned that voting Labour would be voting for what party chairman Chris Patten called the 'double whammy' – higher prices and increased taxation. Labour's sleek and self-assured campaign, designed to persuade voters that the party was responsible enough to be entrusted with power, seemed to bear the Tories out.

FIRST LADIES
The Queen chats to Betty Boothroyd, the Speaker of the House of Commons, as she arrives to open a joint session of both Houses of Parliament in 1995. Boothroyd was the first and is so far the only woman to hold the post of Speaker. She entered Parliament as Labour MP for West Bromwich in 1973 and became deputy speaker of the Commons in 1987. She was elected Speaker in April 1992 by a decisive 134-vote majority over Peter Brooke, a former secretary of state for Northern Ireland. Forthright and funny, she had been a dancer with the Tiller Girls, Britain's most celebrated chorus line, before pursuing her political career. She enjoyed considerable cross-party support while in office as the Speaker, and one of the reasons for her popularity was her obvious devotion to the House of Commons and its traditions. 'The Commons has never been just a career', she told an interviewer. 'It's my life.' Noted for her fair-mindedness, she once reminded the Commons that her role was 'to ensure that the holders of an opinion, however unpopular, are allowed to put across their point of view.' Since her retirement in October 2000, no-one has managed to fill her shoes as Speaker in such a satisfying manner.

'I believe that the Community has made a unique contribution to the development of post-war Europe. Our future is as a European power.'

John Major, speaking in the House of Commons, December 1991

WRONG SIGNALS
It is hard to imagine a scenario more likely to put a British voter off than the final pre-election rally staged by Labour in Sheffield a week before the polls opened. Here, Neil Kinnock salutes the crowd of Labour supporters as if victory is already in his grasp. The applause from deputy leader Roy Hattersley (left) and John Prescott (right) seems less than convinced. Many felt that Kinnock's performance that night played a part in turning uncommitted voters away from Labour, but other commentators insist it had little effect and that Labour's support was already failing. Whatever its effect, the fact remains that John Major and the Tories won a fourth consecutive election victory with a record 14 million votes, beating the previous record vote held by Labour since 1951, when Clement Attlee lost to Churchill's Conservatives.

As the electoral battle gathered momentum, people warmed to Major. When he confessed, rather implausibly, that his favourite place to eat was the roadside restaurant chain Happy Eater, many people felt that they could identify with him. He made a virtue out of his sheer ordinariness. In contrast, the public were not so sure about Neil Kinnock. The Labour leader had made tremendous efforts to modernise the Labour Party, cultivating a statesmanlike, middle-of-the-road image, but he had to fight a largely hostile press as well as the left-wing elements within his party. Many people remained doubtful about whether he was up to the job of Prime Minister – or whether Labour really had turned over a new leaf.

Then, a week before Britain went to the polls, Kinnock made a personal mistake. At the Party's final pre-election rally in Sheffield, presented with a razzmatazz more familiar in US-style political campaigning, he let his enthusiasm run away with him. As he took to the stage to introduce the members of his shadow cabinet by the titles he fondly believed they would hold after the election, he punched the air shouting 'We're alright, we're alright', sounding more like an ageing rock singer than a potential Prime Minister. It was not his finest hour, and the rally as a whole hit the wrong chord with the public. Though the opinion polls indicated that Labour were still on course for victory, voters were on the point of changing their minds.

Kinnock's seeming hubris and other Labour slip-ups – notably the stark admission by John Smith, the shadow chancellor, that taxes would have to go up to pay for the increased social spending that was planned – were eagerly seized on by the Tories and their supporters in the tabloid press. *The Sun*, by far the best-selling paper in Britain, was particularly virulent. 'Nightmare on Kinnock Street' was a typical headline. On the day of the election, its front page was a masterpiece. A large picture of Neil Kinnock's head inside a light bulb was accompanied by the headline: 'If Kinnock wins today, will the last person to leave Britain turn out the lights!'

On election night, it was soon clear that Labour were heading for their fourth defeat in a row. The Conservatives under John Major polled more than 14 million votes, the highest total the party – indeed any party – has ever recorded, although the way the vote split and the country's first-past-the-post system meant that Major only won a majority of 21 seats. Less than half the working class had voted Labour. Kinnock promptly resigned the Labour Party leadership. He was succeeded by John Smith, who lasted for just two years before tragically dying from a heart attack at the early age of 55.

'For every couple of voters who gave us the credit for transforming policies and conduct, there was one who thought the changes were opportunistic and shallow.'

Neil Kinnock, on losing the 1992 general election

WHAT DOES THE CONSERVATIVE PARTY OFFER A WORKING CLASS KID FROM BRIXTON?

THEY MADE HIM PRIME MINISTER.

No wonder John Major believes everyone should have an equal opportunity.

CONSERVATIVE ☒

SELLING THE IMAGE

Astutely, the Conservatives made great play of John Major's humble origins during the 1992 election, winning a sizeable portion of the working-class vote. Mild-mannered, unassuming and likeable, his decision to take to the stump and address crowds from a soap box was also a great success. As a throwback to the past, it pressed the nostalgia button, and compared to Labour's glitzy campaign, it put across the message that the Conservatives were more frugal with money. That was a reputation they would lose within months of the election.

A NEW VOICE

Oscar-winning actress Glenda Jackson found a new role to play when she won the Hampstead and Highgate seat for Labour in the 1992 election. In an impassioned maiden speech in the House of Commons she called on the Prime Minister to make the 'ladders of opportunity' of which he had boasted in the election campaign available to all. They 'must be based', she said, 'on the solid building blocks of education, training, health care free at the point of delivery, and, perhaps most important of all, decent affordable housing.' She also registered her opposition to the government's decision to reintroduce the Asylum Bill to tighten up the grounds on which refugees fleeing to Britain could claim political asylum.

FINANCIAL PANIC
A foreign exchange dealer in London shouts orders down the telephone on 16 September, 1992, soon to be known as 'Black Wednesday'. With the pound under severe pressure on the foreign exchange markets, the Chancellor had just announced a 2 per cent rise in interest rates, to 12 per cent, in an attempt to stem the tide. Later that same day, the panic-stricken attempt to prop up sterling would bring yet another hike in interest rates – to 15 per cent. At the same time, Prime Minister Major had authorised the Bank of England to spend its foreign reserves buying up the sterling that everyone else was busy selling. It was all to no avail. That evening, as the pound was forced out of the ERM, Major, Lamont and the rest of the government suffered a complete humiliation.

BLACK WEDNESDAY

The ball now appeared to be at John Major's feet, but instead of running forward with it, he scored a devastating own goal. In retrospect, the financial crisis that became known as 'Black Wednesday' was probably the key factor that doomed his premiership. On 16 September, 1992, despite all the brave words and promises from Major and Norman Lamont, the pound was forced to withdraw from the European Exchange Rate Mechanism (ERM). It was a shattering blow from which the government never fully recovered.

It had all started two years previously when John Major, then serving as Chancellor of the Exchequer, had finally persuaded a reluctant Margaret Thatcher

continued on page 58

END OF THE ROAD FOR THE CHANCELLOR
The only people who did well out of the crisis were the speculators, led by George Soros (left), who reputedly made more than $1 billion betting against the pound. He became widely known as 'the man who broke the Bank of England.' The day after Black Wednesday UK interest rates went back down to 10 per cent, where they had been before the crisis blew up. By the end of January 1993, Chancellor Lamont had lowered interest rates to 6 per cent, their lowest level since 1977. The dealers on the floor of the London International Financial Futures and Options Exchange (below) are signalling their options in the light of this move. By this time, the economy was recovering quite well, but Norman Lamont's credibility as Chancellor was in tatters. In May, Major removed him from the Treasury and replaced him with Kenneth Clarke.

WHERE ARE WE EXPECTED TO GO ? WHEN IT'S A CRIME TO BE HOMELESS

FROM BAD TO WORSE
A protester at a demonstration against the Criminal Justice and Public Order Bill (above), introduced by the Conservatives in 1994, makes the point that clauses in the legislation would make life even more difficult for the homeless. The changes proposed by Home Secretary Michael Howard – notably

turning squatting and disruptive trespassing from civil into criminal offences – were widely seen as punitive sanctions that in practice might be applied indiscriminately. There was no disputing the fact that a serious housing problem existed and had been getting worse in recent years. This photograph taken at Christmas 1992 (right)

shows homeless people queueing for a meal at one of the seasonal shelters run by Crisis. Nor was homelessness always so publicly visible. There were the so-called 'hidden homeless' – people, mainly women, who lived on friends' and relatives' floors until they had outstayed their welcome. Many were victims of domestic

violence. One woman recounted how she had lived 'with a man who battered me … so I moved to Exeter because I thought I had friends here, but ended up sleeping in a bus station'. She was just one of the city's quota of rough sleepers, who settled down for the night in graveyards, parks, sheds, squats and skips

ON THE STREETS

The recession of the early 1990s added to the problems already facing Britain's have-nots, chief among them being the risk of homelessness and the difficulty of finding a place to live. In London alone, an estimated 20,000 were living in accommodation set aside by charities and housing associations for single homeless people. The number of people sleeping rough on the streets rose sharply and many of these rough-sleepers were just teenagers. New legislation prevented 16 and 17-year-olds from claiming housing benefit, so if they could not live in the family home, they were often left with no real alternative.

'When I came from Africa, I couldn't believe that people could be homeless in Britain. But I discovered that homelessness is a way of life.'

Jeff Motunde, social worker

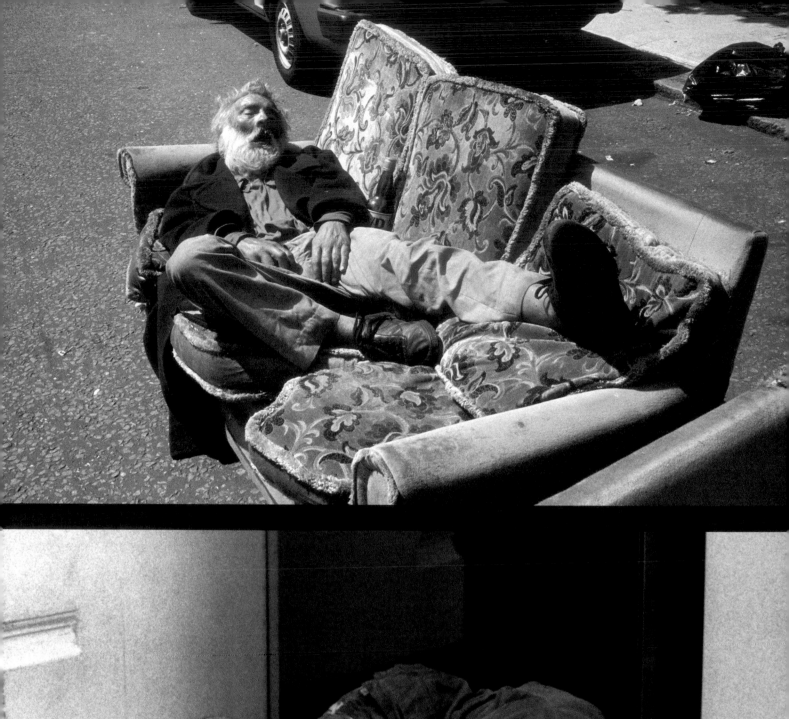

A homeless old man is out for
the count (top left), having
siezed the opportunity offered
by a decrepit sofa thrown out
on a London street to have a
comfortable sleep in the sun.
It was more common to see
people sleeping on the ground
in doorways, like this young
man in Leicester Square
(bottom left). Many turned to
begging in an attempt to find
enough money to pay for a
snack, a hot drink, or a cheap
bed for the night in a hostel. If
they could get away with it,
inside a London Underground
station was a favoured location
(right), as it had the added
advantage of being dry, but they
ran the constant risk of being
moved on by officials or, even
worse, being arrested.

In 1991 John Bird, who had
experienced homelessness for
real himself, launched *The Big
Issue* to highlight the appalling
extent of the problem and to
offer a practical means to get
people off the streets and back
into paid work and a home. The
weekly magazine was sold by
homeless people themselves.
Each *Big Issue* seller, like the
man below, bought copies of
the magazine which they sold
on to the public, pocketing
50 per cent of the cover price.
Many homeless people took up
the challenge, pleased for the
chance to make a little money.

to allow sterling to join the ERM – Europe's fixed-rate currency exchange system. Like the other currencies in the ERM, the pound was pegged against the Deutschmark, the strongest currency in Europe. Sterling's exchange rate was set at DM 2.95 to the pound.

The idea was that being part of the ERM would help Britain to win the battle against inflation, and at first inflation did indeed come down. But several factors began to work against the arrangement, not least the re-unification of Germany, the expense of which encouraged the Bundesbank to keep German interest rates high. In late summer 1992 the pound began to drift downwards in value, as money flowed out of sterling and into Deutschmarks. The Italian lira had the same problem. On 13 September, the lira became the first currency to be forced out of the ERM by speculative pressure. The pound was to follow only three days later.

On 16 September – 'Black Wednesday', as it almost immediately became known – a tidal wave of selling on the foreign exchange markets drove the value of the pound ever further downwards. The government leapt to its defence, declaring there would be no surrender to the speculators. Just a few days earlier, Major had denounced such an option as 'a betrayal of our future.' In a frantic attempt to support sterling's exchange value, he and Norman Lamont authorised two emergency rises in interest rates – the first, that morning, from 10 to 12 per cent and the second, that afternoon, from 12 to 15 per cent. Meanwhile, the Bank of England was digging deep into the nation's foreign currency reserves in its effort to prop up sterling – it is estimated that the day cost the bank around £3.3 billion.

> ## 'I implemented every measure that I could to defend sterling's position … but we faced a unique and ultimately irresistible set of circumstances.'
>
> **Norman Lamont, attempting to explain the financial fiasco to the House of Commons, on 24 September, 1992**

Admitting defeat

It was all in vain. That evening, a white-faced Norman Lamont announced that the government was suspending British membership of the ERM and allowing the pound to float to its own level against the Deutschmark. It was devaluation in all but name. Lamont tried to brush aside the scale of the defeat. Not only did he 'regret nothing', he told the media, but he actually had been 'singing in his bath' the night the news broke. No one found this even slightly amusing.

A RIGHT ROYAL MESS

If the government was having a bad year, the royal family was having a worse one. In her Christmas broadcast, the Queen acknowledged to the whole nation that 1992 had been for her a 'sombre year' – her *annus horribilis*. It had seen the break-up of two of her sons' marriages, her daughter's divorce and, to cap it all, a

MAKING THE BEST OF IT
With three of her children's marriages in disarray, the Queen grimly faced the fact that relationships within her most immediate family were disintegrating. At least Prince Andrew and Sarah Ferguson, the Duke and Duchess of York, parted amicably. They are seen here (above) with their two daughters, Beatrice and Eugenie, at the Royal Windsor Horse Show in May 1992, in what was their first public appearance together since their separation. They remained good friends and continued to share the same home even after their divorce in May 1996.

fire that badly damaged Windsor Castle. It was small wonder that she appeared somewhat grim. The Queen's troubles had started in March, when Buckingham Palace ended weeks of press speculation by tersely confirming that the Duke and Duchess of York had decided to separate. The wording of the announcement made it clear that it was the Duchess who had initiated the separation.

The hope was that the announcement would put a stop to further speculation, but the Palace could not have got it more wrong. In August, the *Daily Mirror* published embarrassing pictures of the Duchess apparently embracing John Bryan, a Texas businessman, beside a swimming pool while on holiday in the south of France. In one of the photographs Bryan appeared to be sucking the Duchess' toes. It was all terribly tacky, but there was worse to come.

A RELATIONSHIP ON THE ROCKS
The body language says it all in this
photograph of the Prince and Princess of
Wales on the last royal tour they undertook
together – to South Korea in November
1992. Their marriage had been under strain
for several years and by this time the
unhappy couple were barely speaking.
Earlier in the year, the Prince had been
infuriated by Andrew Morton's sensational
Diana: Her True Story, even though the
Princess indignantly denied having
cooperated in any way with the author.
In December, it fell to John Major to make
the announcement that the couple were
to separate. In the public relations battle
that followed, Diana won hands down.

A loveless marriage

For some time, rumours had been rife that the marriage of the Prince and Princess of Wales was in trouble, but the Palace had always shrugged off such claims. It was different that May when *Diana: Her True Story* hit the streets. The book's contents were sensational and it became an instant best-seller. Though the author Andrew Morton was at pains to point out that the Princess had not helped him to write the book, it was widely thought to be an accurate reflection of her feelings. Morton claimed that the Princess was trapped in a loveless marriage, unsupported by her unsympathetic husband, who had taken up again with his old flame Camilla Parker Bowles. Unable to cope with the pressures of royal life, Diana had developed a major eating disorder and, Morton further claimed, had contemplated killing herself at least five times over the past few years.

For all those who had taken the fairytale Princess to their hearts, the revelations were shocking. Morton's book blue the lid off what the royals had taken such pains to conceal. The relationship between Prince and Princess was exposed as a sham. Belatedly, the Palace urged the Press Complaints Commission to condemn the media coverage of the troubled marriage, which it duly did: 'The most recent intrusive and speculative treatment by sections of the press and indeed by broadcasters of the marriage of the Prince and Princess of Wales is an odious example of journalists dabbling their fingers in the stuff of other people's souls.' Michael Shea, the Queen's Press Secretary, went further, denouncing the tabloid press as 'a cancer in the soft underbelly of the nation'. The media took no notice. Tapes featuring intimate conversations between the Princess and James Gilbey and between the Prince and Camilla Parker Bowles were hawked around Fleet Street. Eventually, their contents were splashed all over the papers.

The game was up. After a disastrous tour of Korea, during which the royal couple barely spoke, it was obvious to everyone that the situation could not go on. Leak followed leak into the papers as the Prince and Princess became embroiled in what became nicknamed 'the war of the Wales's'. Even the Queen's personal intervention failed to calm things. On 6 November, the Palace finally admitted that there was a rift in the marriage and on 9 December, 1992, the couple's official separation was announced.

Taxing times

The Princess's popularity now rose to new heights, while that of Charles – and the rest of the Royal Family – plummeted to new lows. To add to the Queen's woes, resentful voices were raised at the government's decision to pay for the restoration of Windsor Castle following the fire there in November. The Queen, they argued, could afford to foot the bill herself. Opinion polls indicated that 90 per cent of Britons thought that the Queen should pay taxes and that state payments to other royals should be cut out altogether.

The Queen agreed to all three demands. She offered to meet 70 per cent of the cost of restoration at Windsor, volunteered to pay tax from the following year and said that, in future, only she, the Prince of Wales and the Queen Mother would receive state money from the Civil List. She would provide for the other members of the sprawling Windsor clan herself. These were major concessions, though the Queen had been considering volunteering to pay tax for some time in advance of the public pressure. It was small wonder that she and her family looked forward to a better year to follow. So, too, did John Major, but he was to be disappointed.

UP IN FLAMES

On 20 November, 1992 – the Queen and Prince Philip's 45th wedding anniversay – Windsor Castle went up in flames. Next to Sandringham and Balmoral, it was the Queen's favourite residence. It was a dreadful end to a dreadful year.

The blaze is thought to have been started by a spotlight too close to a curtain in the Queen's Private Chapel. Re-wiring work was being undertaken in some of the State Rooms at the time. The flames spread swiftly and by the time fire-fighters got the blaze under control, more than 100 rooms had been damaged, including St George's Hall. It took 250 firemen 15 hours and 1.5 million gallons of water to put the fire out. At the height of the fire, 39 fire-fighting appliances were employed. Members of the royal household and others were involved in rescuing as many valuables as possible – paintings, clocks, ornaments, furniture. The one piece of good fortune was that no one was killed.

In the aftermath, the big question was who would pay the bill for the repairs. Though the government initially said that the taxpayer would foot the restoration bill, the announcement stirred up considerable public hostility. Eventually, the Queen offered to pay 70 per cent of the cost herself. The final bill came in at £37 million.

JOHN MAJOR'S INNINGS

When he came to power John Major aspired to create 'a nation at ease with itself', but as his term in office progressed it seemed to most people that what emerged was anything but. The fiasco of Black Wednesday led to a collapse of respect for him and his government early in his administration. IRA bombers brought terror back to the mainland, striking in Warrington and at the heart of the City of London. In Parliament, the Conservative Party tore itself to pieces as Eurosceptics within its ranks rebelled against their leader's attempts to ratify the Maastricht Treaty. And then there was the Prime Minister's own ill-fated call for a return to family values, which was to be so thoroughly undermined by sleaze among Tory MPs. Major found himself beset by dissent at every turn.

A FINE DAY OUT The gap between rich and poor widened under John Major's administration. By the time these picnickers were photographed at Henley Regatta in July 1997, the public's confidence in Major had evaporated and Tony Blair had replaced him in power.

LIVING THROUGH CHANGE

There was no doubt that Britain was changing fast in the 1990s. For one thing, people were turning away from organised religion as never before. By 1995, the adult membership of the Church of England had fallen to 1,785,000, while the number of confirmations dwindled from 190,713 in 1960 to only 40,881 in 1997. It was reckoned that churches were closing at the rate of about one a week. Nor was the decline confined to the Anglican church. Between 1970 and 1995, the Trinitarian churches lost around a third of their members, the Roman Catholics 29 per cent, the Presbyterians 33 per cent and the Methodists 38 per cent. In contrast, non-Christian religions were flourishing. Thanks largely to immigration and a higher-than-average birth rate, by 1995 there were more Muslims in the country than Methodists.

Gamely, the Church of England tried to battle against the tide. Much to the horror of some, services were modernised and in 1994 the first women priests were ordained. The traditionalists were appalled and some expressed their discontent in words that were perhaps less than Christian. 'You can no more ordain a woman than a pork pie', said one. 'Swamped by modernity, liberalism and feminism, the Church of England is now nothing more than a rotting carcass', lamented another. Some 400 male priests quit in protest. The fact, though, was that most people did not really care.

Shopping, sex and marriage

After many centuries of being a Christian country, Britain was rapidly becoming a secular nation. The Sunday Trading Act, which came into force in August 1994, seemed symptomatic of this drift towards secularism. With certain restrictions, the Act allowed shops in England and Wales to open (in Scotland it was custom, rather than the law, the kept shops closed on the Sabbath). The move upset many – and not just Church-goers – who felt that Sunday should remain special, but the numbers spoke for themselves. By the latter part of the decade just over a million people attended Church of England services on Sundays, compared to 11 million who went shopping. In terms of sales per hour, the day became Sainsbury's busiest of the week.

Marriage, too, seemed to be going out of fashion. One reason for this was that more women were going out to work than ever before, carving out their own careers and earning more into the bargain. They saw no reason why they should surrender the independence that had been gained over the previous three decades. The sexual climate had changed dramatically. Young people in particular seemed to have broken the link between sex and marriage and were starting their sex lives earlier, while putting off getting married until later. For the majority, the traditional constraint of 'no sex before marriage' belonged to the past.

The belief in marriage as a lifetime commitment, as reflected in the wedding vow 'till death do us part', also seemed to have gone the same way. By the middle of the decade, the figures showed one out of every two marriages ending in separation. Divorce had long ceased to be the prerogative of the rich. It now became easier to obtain. In 1971, there were 296,000 divorced women in England and Wales; by 2000, the figure had risen to a phenomenal 2,063,000.

CHURCH REVOLUTION
A group of female deacons share a laugh outside Bristol Cathedral before their ordination into the Anglican priesthood on 12 March, 1994. They were among the first group of 32 women who were ordained on that historic day. The decision to allow women to become priests was a milestone in Church of England history. It had taken 17 years of heated debate within the Church to reach a decision to make the change, and even then the necessary legislation was passed in the General Synod by just two votes. Traditionalists found it hard to accept the change. Government minister Ann Widdecombe, who left the Church and converted to Roman Catholicism over the issue, accused Anglican leaders of 'promoting political correctness above the very clear teachings of Scripture'. The Reverend Peter Geldard, another prominent opponent, warned that the decision would 'pit diocese against diocese, parish against parish and parishioner against parishioner'.

'What binds us together in God's love as a Church is vastly more important than a disagreement about women's ordination.'

Dr George Carey, Archbishop of Canterbury, 1994

UNITED WE STAND
Transport union leader Jimmy Knapp, wearing the light raincoat (left), heads a TUC protest march against government plans to close 31 of the nation's remaining coal pits. Outwardly, the TUC presented a united front in supporting the miners to fight the cuts, but in private it counselled the miners' leaders against attempting another full-scale confrontation with government.

Trade unions in decline

Trades unions, too, were on the wane. Tory legislation had whittled away at their powers – the main changes were the virtual abolition of the closed shop and restraints placed on strike action and picketing – but the real reasons for union decline were more deep-rooted. Partly it was due to the rise in unemployment over the previous decade, but this in turn was the result of a fundamental change in the type of work available. The decline of Britain's traditional heavy industries had rapidly gained pace under Margaret Thatcher and this trend now continued: between 1979 and 1999, they lost 40 per cent of their union membership.

The miners were the worst hit. Between 1985 and 1990, as 94 out of 170 of the nation's pits closed, the National Union of Mineworkers lost 80 per cent of its membership. In 1992, as a prelude to privatisation, Michael Heseltine announced the closure of 31 more pits at a cost of another 30,000 jobs, sparking off long and furious protests. Richard Alexander, the Conservative MP for a Nottinghamshire mining constituency, bitterly opposed the closures, speaking of a 'wave of anger sweeping across north Nottinghamshire such as I have never known before'. The long reign of 'King Coal' was drawing painfully to its close.

Mining was not the only traditional industry in deep trouble. Shipbuilding was in much the same state, as were iron and steel. Even the once prosperous car industry was expiring. When Austin Rover was sold to the German automobile giant BMW in 1994, the nation lost its last British-owned mass car-maker.

From Old Labour to New

The political influence of the unions was dwindling, too. The days of beer and sandwiches in Downing Street were long gone, but now Labour reformers set out to tackle the dominant position of the unions within the party – even though it relied on union subscriptions for 90 per cent of its funds.

continued on page 73

NEW LABOUR MOVEMENT
A pensive Gordon Brown (right), shadow chancellor of the exchequer, presiding over a press conference in September 1993. Brown had first entered Parliament as Labour MP for Dunfermline East against the tide of Margaret Thatcher's landslide victory in 1983. In the Commons he found himself sharing an office with another newly elected MP – Tony Blair. In May 1994, after the untimely death of Labour leader John Smith, Brown and Blair, who by then was shadow home secretary, emerged as the two leading contenders for the succession. Indeed, many expected Brown to succeed Smith, but in the event Blair emerged as the favourite and Brown decided not to stand against him in the leadership contest. Rumour had it that they had come to a secret agreement over dinner in a fashionable Islington restaurant by which Blair would get first shot at the premiership, then stand aside later for Brown. And in the meantime, Brown would have virtual autonomy at the Treasury.

THE MINERS' LAST STAND

The final battle to keep Britain's deep coal mines open came to a head in 1992, when John Major's government announced plans to close a third of them with the consequent loss of around 30,000 jobs. In many mining communities the pit was the sole employer and the stark message for the government from this woman (right), photographed at a protest demonstration held in London in October 1992, is that when the pit is lost, the whole community is lost. The miner (far right) was photographed in April 1993 as he and colleagues from Houghton Main colliery lobbied Parliament against the closure plans. The emotion visible in both their faces – and on the face of backbench MP Dennis Skinner, seen here (bottom) at the October rally – is not anger but sadness.

Arthur Scargill, the fiery president of the National Union of Mineworkers, announced that he would fight the cuts to the finish, but after losing the bitter year-long struggle against Mrs Thatcher's government in 1985, the miners no longer had any real power to resist. Though Neil Clarke, chairman of British Coal, described the cuts as 'grievous', they were seen by many as inevitable. Even the TUC, though it publicly backed the miners, was privately lukewarm in its support. In the Labour Party out-and-out advocates of all-out resistance, such as Dennis Skinner, were in a distinct minority, especially when the government made it clear that any form of industrial action would dramatically reduce the amount of money they were prepared to offer miners facing redundancy. As a result, many miners felt just as betrayed by the Labour Party and the TUC as by Major's government. The anger of these protesters (far right) was directed not at government ministers but at Labour and TUC speakers at a rally held in London in March 1993. The protests made no difference, and the decline of Britain's coal-mining industry continued, with other closures following on after the 31 proposed pits had closed.

WHEN THEY CLOSE A PIT

THEY KILL A COMMUNITY

'I did not join the Labour Party to protest. I joined it as a party of government and I will make sure that it is a party of government.'

Tony Blair, 1995

A MAN WITH AMBITION
Tony Blair, seen here with his wife Cherie and their three children in the garden of his Sedgefield constituency home in Trimdon Colliery, Durham. Blair was young, personable and compelling. Even media magnate Rupert Murdoch, a long-time Tory supporter, was favourably impressed. 'I could see people voting for him', Murdoch told Piers Morgan, then editor of the *News of the World*. 'He's a breath of fresh air.' Even after his election to the party leadership, there were many both inside and outside the Labour Party who were unclear exactly what it was that Tony Blair stood for. One thing they did know was that he was against Clause IV of the Labour Party constitution and he was determined to be rid of it.

Up until the end of the 1980s, the unions controlled five out of every six votes at Labour Party conferences, largely through the exercise of what was termed the block vote. They also held two thirds of the seats – 18 out of 29 – on the party's National Executive. This was all to change. At the Labour Party conference of 1990 it was agreed in principle that future parliamentary candidates should be selected on the basis of one member, one vote. Three years later John Smith, in his first conference as party leader, put his political future on the line by demanding that the constitution be revised accordingly. By a narrow majority, he got his way: the selection of all parliamentary candidates would be determined by the votes of individual members, while the use of the block vote at party conferences would be markedly reduced. The procedures for the election of the leader and deputy leader of the party were to be reformed as well.

It was a giant step forward for the modernisers within the Labour Party, which had not yet been remodelled by them as New Labour. How far Smith would have gone along with them will never by known, for on 12 May, 1994, he suffered a massive heart attack and died. In the leadership election triggered by Smith's death, Tony Blair won handsomely, beating John Prescott into second place with Margaret Beckett, who had been deputy leader to Smith, coming third.

'You don't look or sound like a Labour MP' was ex-Tory leader Edward Heath's blunt summing up when he was introduced to Blair in the House of Commons. Blair certainly stood to the right of his predecessor. He soon proved himself to be a disciplined, focused political operator. Determined to modernise his party root and branch, he started by scrapping one of the most contentious clauses in its constitution.

Getting rid of Clause Four

Ever since 1918, when the Labour Party adopted into its constitution Sidney Webb's wording of 'Aims and Values', Clause Four had pledged that Labour would strive for 'common ownership of the means of production' to 'secure for the workers by hand or by brain the full fruit of their industry'. In a word, the clause meant nationalisation, and generally speaking Labour governments since the Second World War had done just that. Now, in a world where communism had fallen and the Berlin Wall had been dismantled, the clause seemed to many to be distinctly out of date, although for some in the Labour Party it remained a fundamental expression of their socialist beliefs.

'I do like Blair, he sounds so dynamic compared to Major and his ghastly old bores.'

Piers Morgan, from his diaries, October 1994

PUBLIC PROTEST

The 1990s kicked off with demonstrations against the community charge – the poll tax, as it was better known. It ended with mass protests against British military involvement in conflicts in places as far afield as the Balkans, Iraq and Sierra Leone. As the decade progressed, more and more people seemed ready to get involved in 'direct action' with varied objectives. So-called eco-warriors, claiming to be acting 'against cars, roads and the system supporting them', waged a long but ultimately unsuccessful battle against the building of the M3 extension across Twyford Down, one of the most beautiful parts of Hampshire. And each year, growing numbers of gays flocked to the capital to take part in the Gay Pride march.

FRIENDS OF THE EARTH
A travelling musician poses for the camera during the protest against the Newbury bypass in 1996 (right). Members of Green groups came from all over the country to try to stop the road development, setting up camp on the site, building tunnels and tree houses and using themselves as human shields to stop security guards and diggers gaining access to the route. The protest lasted well into the following year; during it, more than 1,000 people were arrested. Not all demonstrations were so confrontational. The smiling demonstrator below is taking part in a legalise cannabis rally outside Parliament in 1998. In the brave new world of Blair, some were optimistic that Britain's drug laws – at least in the case of cannabis – might be relaxed.

IT'S OKAY TO BE GAY

A pink tank makes a splash at the 1995 Gay Pride march in London (above); the rainbow flags were the internationally recognised symbol of the Gay Liberation movement. The lesbian couple (left) have eyes solely for each other on the 1993 Gay Pride demonstration. The first gay marches in the capital had taken place in

November 1970, when 150 gay men walked through Highbury Fields in the north of the city. The first official British Gay Pride rally was held two years later, in July 1972, with around 2,000 people participating.

It had been a long, uphill struggle for gays and lesbians to win recognition of their sexuality and the right to be respected. Though the private practice of

homosexuality between consenting adult men had been legalised in 1967 – it had never been specifically illegal for women – there was still a long way to go before social attitudes towards gays changed and the right to be homosexual won general public acceptance. For years, many gays continued to live in fear of public exposure and ridicule. Sometimes,

though, the response was surprising. Matthew Parris, now a prominent newspaper columnist but formerly a young Conservative backbencher, recalled how he plucked up the courage to come out and tell Mrs Thatcher that he was gay. She laid a sympathetic hand on his wrist and murmured 'That must have been very hard for you, dear.'

WHO NEEDS THE BOMB?
Protesters hang an anti-Trident banner over Westminster Bridge, as police in a patrol boat look on. Calls for Britain to give up its nuclear weapons gained pace during the decade as Trident missiles, with which its Vanguard submarines were equipped, started to approach the end of their useful operational life. Replacing them would cost billions. But New Labour, which had ditched the previous Labour pledge to dump the nuclear deterrent, proved as stubbornly resistant to anti-nuclear protests as its Tory predecessors had been.

'To replace Trident ... would be a complete waste of money, because there are no circumstances in which we would use it independently.'

Professor Stephen Hawking

STOP THE BOMBING
Anti-war marchers protest in 1999 against the NATO bombing of Serbia, aimed at halting ethnic cleansing in Kosovo. In ordering the RAF to join the US Air Force in bombing Belgrade, the Serb capital, Blair said the aim was 'crystal clear … to curb Slobodan Milosevic's ability to wage war on an innocent civilian population'. The RAF had already joined the Americans in bombing targets in Iraq in an attempt to destroy Saddam Hussein's supposed weapons of mass destruction.

Blair believed that Clause IV was responsible for Labour losing election after election. He was not the first in the party to think so. Hugh Gaitskell, party leader from 1955 to 1963, had attempted to reform the clause after losing the election in 1959. He lost the argument on Clause IV, too, and left-wingers in the party raised its status to Sacred Cow. Tony Blair began his assault in 1993, but it was at his first conference as leader that he persuaded the party it had to go. At a special conference the following spring, he unveiled his alternative – the somewhat anodyne and deliberately unobjectionable promise to create 'a community in which power, wealth and opportunity are in the hands of the many not the few'.

The change was symptomatic of a decisive shift in the balance of power in favour of New Labour and would be reinforced in phrasing and sentiment at every opportunity. In his conference speech, Blair used the word 'new' 59 times, while referring to socialism just once; the working class did not rate a mention at all.

What he actually stood for politically remained obscure, but there was no doubting that he was charismatic, full of personality and highly motivated. He would also turn out to be a master of the instant sound bite. By contrast, Major appeared grey, dull, complacent and boring. At bottom, he was a fundamentally decent man, whose tragedy was to misunderstand so profoundly the changing nature of the nation he led.

MURDER MOST SHOCKING

Britain was no longer, as John Major fondly believed, 'the country of long shadows on cricket grounds, warm beer, invincible green suburbs, dog lovers and pools fillers and, as George Orwell said, "old maids bicycling to holy communion though the morning mist".' It was doubtful it ever had been, but the reality now was of a discontented land in which the social framework seemed not only fragile, but also under considerable stress. Violent crime was inexorably on the rise, but some incidents went beyond the normal conception of crime, hitting a raw nerve revealed by the fractures in society.

On 12 February, 1993, James Bulger, a Merseyside toddler, disappeared from a Bootle shopping centre. His battered body was found two days later beside a railway line in Walton, just two miles from where he had last been seen. The nation was appalled when it emerged he had been abducted and brutally murdered by two ten-year-old boys, who were arrested, charged and convicted.

In April the same year, an 18-year-old black schoolboy called Stephen Lawrence was simply waiting for a bus in Eltham, south London, when he was viciously attacked and stabbed to death by a gang of white youths. The attack was completely unprovoked and, as was clear from the start, was racially motivated.

The killers of James Bulger were brought to justice relatively quickly. The same could not be said in the Stephen Lawrence case. Though police investigators were certain that they knew who had committed the crime, no one was brought to court for the murder: the Crown Prosecution Service said it lacked the hard evidence to secure a conviction. Eventually, the parents of the murdered teenager brought a private prosecution against the five white youths who were the prime

HOUSE OF HORRORS
In March 1994 a police investigator leaves 25 Cromwell Street, Gloucester, carrying a crate of potential evidence. Two uniformed officers stand guard at the gate of the home of Fred and Rose West. In February 1994 Fred West was arrested on suspicion of having murdered one of their daughters, Heather, who had disappeared some years earlier. Rose was arrested in April, as the police investigation began to reveal the full horror of their crimes. By the time this photograph was taken of a police team digging up the Wests' garden (top right), nine female bodies had been discovered, three of them mutilated. Heather's body was among them. The couple were eventually charged with the murder of ten young women over a period of more than ten years. One of the first to die was Mary Bastholm, a pretty 15-year-old whom West had abducted from a bus stop in Gloucester. Her rape, torture and murder set the pattern for many of West's subsequent homicides. The couple also killed several of their lodgers and some of the nannies they had persuaded to come and look after their own children.

suspects. It failed after the evidence of a key eyewitness was ruled inadmissible. It was not until 1997 that an inquest was held. The five suspects were summoned to give evidence, but refused to answer any questions on the grounds that they might incriminate themselves. The next day, the *Daily Mail* named the young men involved, challenging them, if they were innocent, to sue for libel. 'It is no light matter', the paper declared, 'when a national newspaper condemns as murderers five men who have never been convicted in court, but when the judicial system has failed so lamentably to deal with the killers of Stephen Lawrence, extraordinary measures are demanded.' Not one of the men sued, but it was a pyrrhic victory for the *Mail* for neither were any of the suspects retried for the murder.

In 1998 an official enquiry into the Lawrence case, headed by High Court judge Sir William Macpherson, was scathing of the police and the slipshod way that the case had been conducted. His report concluded that the Metropolitan force was tainted with 'institutional racism' and that this had hampered their investigations right from the start. It marked the beginning of some soul-searching for the police and an acknowledgment that racist attitudes had to be tackled.

Serial slaughter

In 1994 Frederick West, a 52-year-old builder from Gloucester, and his second wife, Rose, were arrested and charged with multiple murders of girls and young women. The couple turned out to be among the worst serial killers of the century. As the police dug up the cellar floor and garden of their home they unearthed corpse after corpse. The exact number of people tortured and murdered by the Wests has never been established, but it is believed that at least 22 young women and girls – possible as many as 30 – died at their hands.

Fred West committed suicide in his prison cell while waiting to stand trial. He was found hanged by torn-up strips of bed linen on New Year's Day, 1995. His wife, who steadfastly refused to admit her guilt, was left to face the court alone. One of the murders, that of her step-daughter Charmaine West, was pinpointed to a time when Fred West was in prison and other evidence, too, pointed to her being far more than an unwilling accomplice. In October 1995 Rose West was found guilty of ten murders and sentenced to ten terms of life imprisonment. The trial judge recommended that she never be released. The infamous 'House of Horrors' was demolished – every brick was crushed and every timber burned to deter souvenir-hunters – and the site was turned into a landscaped pathway.

Massacre in Dunblane

The Wests were clearly mentally twisted. So, too, was Thomas Hamilton, who on 13 March, 1996, perpetrated the worst multiple killing in British history. The apparently motiveless slaughter took place in the Scottish village of Dunblane, just north of Stirling. That morning, armed with four hand-guns, Hamilton burst into the gymnasium of the local primary school and opened fire on the class of mainly five-year-olds there. He moved on and continued shooting in the playground and in a school corridor, then returned to the gymnasium and turned one of the guns on himself. The massacre lasted just three minutes. Hamilton had killed 16 children and a teacher who tried to protect them.

The nation was shocked into silence. As Piers Morgan, editor of the *Daily Mirror,* wrote in his diary, 'to deliberately target children like this is just beyond belief'. The front page of the *Mirror* the next day captured the horrific extend of the tragedy. It showed each of the dead children's faces, positioned in squares bordering the perimeter of the page, with a photograph of Hamilton in the centre. The stark headline read: 'He Killed Them All.'

STRIVING FOR PEACE

There was no way, of course, that Major and his government could prevent such terrible random crimes. But there was something that the Prime Minister was determined to do – to try to put an end to the continuing violence in Northern Ireland. Taking his political life in his hands, he embarked on what had hitherto been considered unthinkable. He started talking to the Provisional IRA.

On 15 December, 1993, came what was officially termed the Joint Declaration on Peace, which quickly became better known as the Downing Street Declaration.

continued on page 86

SEEKING A SETTLEMENT

Determined to try to bring peace to Ulster, John Major worked hard to negotiate the so-called Downing Street Declaration with Irish premier Albert Reynolds. The two men are seen here (above) announcing their agreement to the press on 15 December, 1993. The British government declared that it had 'no selfish or strategic interest in Northern Ireland', while in return Reynolds acknowledged that any change in the political status of the northern province would need the full consent of the Protestant majority there.

Though the IRA declared a cease-fire at the end of August the following year, all attempts to take the peace process forward from there failed. The Loyalists were in no mood to tolerate further concessions, while the IRA resolutely refused to decommission its arms. There was no bridging the gap between the two sides. Loyalist paramilitaries, as depicted in the partly obscured graffiti seen on this house wall (right), would continue to enjoy support in the eastern part of Belfast. Ulster boys like these would have to wait more years before playing football against a background of peace.

BACK TO BOMBS
A paratrooper watches the changing of the guard at Buckingham Palace (top right) as part of the security clampdown following the end of the IRA ceasefire in February 1996. The IRA had resumed its mainland bombing, striking first at Canary Wharf, the symbolic redevelopment project in London's docklands. In the early evening of 9 February a massive bomb exploded near South Quay station, devastating the office block above it (left). Two men in a nearby newsagents were killed and 39 people were injured, most of them by flying glass. The IRA bombers followed this up on 15 June with a huge bomb in Manchester city centre. A successful evacuation prior to the explosion meant that fortunately no-one was killed, but more than 200 people were treated for injuries. Then, on 14 July, the bombers returned to Ulster, destroying the Killyhevlin Hotel in Enniskillen (bottom right). Forty people were injured in the attack, the first in the province since the end of the ceasefire. The people of Enniskillen were no strangers to such atrocities. On 8 November, 1987, an IRA bomb killed 11 people as they paid their respects at the Remembrance Day service. On that occasion even IRA supporters reacted with revulsion. A decade later, on Remembrance Day 1997, Sinn Fein leader Gerry Adams made a formal apology for the bombing.

Appearing outside No.10, Major and Albert Reynolds, the Taoiseach (premier) of the Irish Republic, announced that they had reached agreement on a joint policy to put an end to paramilitary violence and bring about lasting peace. The IRA's response was cautious, but almost immediate. In April 1994, it said it would abide by a three-day truce. Five months later, it announced a complete 'cessation of military operations'. Loyalist paramilitaries followed suit in October.

Many people took this to mean a permanent ceasefire, but they were to be disappointed. On 9 February, 1996, the Provisional IRA declared the ceasefire at an end, claiming that the British government had squandered 'this unprecedented opportunity to resolve the conflict' by refusing to sit down with Sinn Fein, the official republican political party in the north. The mainland bombing campaign resumed with a huge bomb blast in London's Canary Wharf, followed by another in a shopping centre in the heart of Manchester, in which more than 200 people were injured. Major battled on. All-party talks started – without Sinn Fein – but there was a limit to what he could do. By this time, he had lost his independent majority in Parliament and was reliant on the votes of Ulster Unionist MPs.

SPLIT UPON SPLIT

Major's main problem was that the Conservatives were increasingly riddled with internal dissent. The battle started at the party conference in October 1992, in the aftermath of 'Black Wednesday', when every Eurosceptic speaker had been cheered to the echo by the rank-and-file delegates. Over the following months, humiliation followed humiliation as Major struggled to get Parliament to ratify the Treaty of Maastricht and so make it binding. The nadir came the next summer, when Tory rebels made common cause with the Labour Opposition and actually voted for an amendment that would stop ratification unless the treaty's controversial Social Chapter was reinstated. The result of the vote in the House of Commons was a tie. The government was saved only because the Speaker, Betty Boothroyd, followed precedent by casting her deciding vote in its favour.

The European issue was splitting the Tory Party into warring factions and there seemed nothing Major could do to heal the breech. Alan Clark bemoaned the state of affairs in his diary: 'What is happening to the Party? They are now a medieval army in the reign of King Stephen – pre-Ironside – each one concerned to preserve their individual estates (constituencies) fragmenting into even smaller Margravates around dignitaries who may, or may not, be in a position to distribute favours and booty. Discipline has completely broken down, and they loot the countryside as they march and counter-march.'

ALAN CLARK – POLITICAL MAVERICK
Controversial Tory MP Alan Clark poses with his much-loved Jaguar SS100 sports car at Saltwood Castle, his Kent home, in April 1994. At the time of the photograph Clark was between parliamentary seats, having stood down at the 1992 election following Mrs Thatcher's demise and his own involvement in the arms-to-Iraq scandal. He was now trying to win the nomination for Kensington and Chelsea, a constituency newly created by the Boundaries Commission for the 1997 election which would be the safest Tory seat in the country. Clark had owned the car since his undergraduate days at Oxford and his love affair with it had not dimmed. In his diaries he described how, one November lunchtime, he beat a BMW off the lights out of Hyde Park. 'As the lights went amber the faithful SS, always unbeatable for the first 50 feet of a standing start ... was off – the BM was nowhere.' It was typical of Clark's raffish behaviour. A self-confessed self-indulgent egocentric, he became as notorious for his love affairs and his diary as for his right-wing views.

'In office but not in power'

Not everything was the government's fault, but it got all the blame from an unforgiving electorate. Other Cabinet members seemed as accident-prone as their leader. Michael Heseltine announced a plan to sell off local post offices, but a howl of outrage – particularly in country areas – forced him to withdraw the proposal. NHS waiting lists and school class sizes grew due to spending cuts imposed by Kenneth Clarke, who had taken over from Norman Lamont as Chancellor once the Prime Minister plucked up the nerve to sack his one-time close associate. Michael Howard, Clarke's successor as Home Secretary, managed to upset everyone – judges, police and public – when he tried to steamroller controversial law-and-order proposals into law.

It was all symptomatic of a government at bay. Norman Lamont, who had indignantly turned down the post of Secretary of State for the Environment when he was sacked from the Treasury, summed up the situation in a bitter resignation speech. 'We give the impression', he said, 'of being in office but not in power.' Opinion polls, local elections, European elections and by-elections all showed dissatisfaction with Major's performance growing. One poll showed him as having the lowest approval rating of any Prime Minister ever – even lower than Neville Chamberlain's in 1940. With Labour's poll lead soaring to 25 per cent, it seemed as if Conservatism was withering at the roots. True blue Tory seats – Newbury in Berkshire, Christchurch in Hampshire, Wirral South in Cheshire – fell like ninepins to the Liberal Democrats and Labour. The Scottish National Party got into the act as well, its candidate romping home to victory in the 1995 Perth and Kinross by-election. It seemed as if there were no safe havens for the Conservatives anywhere in the kingdom.

Europe, above all, remained a painful thorn in the government's side. People were outraged when French farmers blocked imports of British lamb and veal. The nation's fishermen were furious when the EU cut the quotas for how many and what type of fish could be caught. To add insult to injury, EU policy also allowed Spanish and French fishermen access to what had traditionally been British fishing waters.

Killer cows

Discontent with the EU reached a crescendo in 1996, when an EU blanket ban was slapped on the export of British beef. But for once, the EU had justice on its side. British cattle had become infected with a brain disease called Bovine Spongiform Encethapalopathy (BSE), which soon became better known as 'mad cow disease'. The cause of the disease remains the subject of debate, but the main suspect – and the root cause identified in a subsequent British enquiry – was the inclusion of meat and bone meal as 'added protein' in cattle food, which had led to scrapie, a similar disease in sheep, jumping the species barrier to cattle, another natural herbivore. The inclusion of animal products in cattle food had been made possible following the deregulation of animal feed back in Mrs Thatcher's day.

EMPTY MARKET
Farmers walk through Gloucester cattle market, a major livestock mart, devoid of cattle on 25 March, 1996. The government had just announced new slaughterhouse controls, but had stopped short of ordering the wholesale destruction of cows in an attempt to control so-called 'mad cow' disease, or BSE. It had recently been reported that BSE might be linked to a new variant strain of Creutzfeldt-Jakob Disease (CJD) in the UK. CJD is a brain disorder in humans that is invariably fatal; the new strain had so far claimed ten victims.

BONE OF CONTENTION
The issue of cattle and BSE would not go away. Here, David Cray of the British National Cattle Association delivers a beef rib joint to Downing Street on 15 December, 1997, in protest at a ban on the selling of beef on the bone due to come into effect at midnight. The ban was introduced by the new Labour government, which had come to power that May, following intensive scientific research involving cattle and mice which seemed to indicate a small increased risk of humans being infected by BSE from animal bone tissue. Acknowledging that the measure was precautionary, Dr Jack Cunningham, then Minister for Agriculture, said: 'Notwithstanding that this is a very small risk, I could not accept that even a small risk should be taken. That is the basis on which we have taken this action.' In typical British fashion, many people who had never thought of cooking beef on the bone found it irresistible now that it was illegal and the law was routinely flouted. The ban was lifted almost exactly two years later, on 17 December, 1999.

Initially, government ministers tried to laugh off any notion that BSE posed a threat to human health. As part of the attempt to show the public that British beef was safe to eat, John Selwyn Gummer, the Minister of Agriculture, paraded his four-year-old daughter Cordelia in front of the television cameras and tried to persuade her to eat a beef burger. When the little girl refused, Gummer had to swallow it himself and pronounced the burger 'absolutely delicious'.

Gradually, the belief that humans could not be affected by BSE crumbled in the face of new evidence. Victoria Rimmer, a sparky Welsh teenager, had become the first known victim back in 1993, when she was hospitalised after showing signs of failing memory, fading eye sight, weight loss and general disorientation. Other cases followed. In 1996 Stephen Dorrel, the Secretary of State for Health, was forced to admit to the House of Commons that BSE was 'the most likely explanation at present' to account for ten instances of a new variant strain of Creutzfeldt-Jakob Disease, a fatal degenerative brain disorder. The EU, it seemed, had been right to be concerned.

Belatedly, the government acted. Tough new regulations called for the deboning of beef before it was cooked and eaten, while farmers were ordered to slaughter all beef cattle more than 30 months old. Soon, the countryside of Britain's green and pleasant land was studded with the funeral pyres of cattle; 147,000 animals were destroyed in all. Some said that the stench of burning cattle was symptomatic of the state of Major's administration. Despite official attempts to condemn the EU for overreacting, people at large reckoned the government was more to blame.

SCANDALS AND SLEAZE

There were plenty of other reasons why people were becoming more and more disenchanted with Major, his government and the Conservatives in general. A lurid cocktail of sexual and financial scandals combined to create a general feeling that the administration was not only out of touch, but also tacky and corrupt.

It began in July 1992, when David Mellor, the National Heritage Secretary and self-styled 'Minister for Fun', was exposed as an adulterer. The news that he had been conducting a torrid affair with Antonia de Sanchez, an obscure Spanish actress, was splashed across the tabloid front pages. Mellor toughed out the scandal until September, when further revelations that he had allowed Monica Bauwens, the daughter of a senior member of the Palestine Liberation Organisation, to lend him a holiday villa and even pay for his air tickets finally forced his resignation. He complained bitterly that the press had deliberately

THE MAN WHO BROKE BARINGS

Rogue trader Nick Leeson (right), looking almost relieved, on his way to court in Singapore to be charged with forgery and fraud on 24 November, 1995. The extraordinary story of his activities had become headline news back in February 1995 when Barings Bank – Britain's oldest merchant bank, founded in 1762 – was forced to declare itself insolvent. Traders on the floor of the Singapore International Monetary Exchange – seen above on 27 February, 1995, the day after the news broke – were among the first to panic, especially when the Bank of England made it clear that there would be no bail-out.

Leeson had arrived in Singapore in 1992 to run the Barings office there. It is said to have been covering up a loss caused by a colleague's error that first set him on the slippery slope that would end with him committing theft and fraud on an almost unimaginable scale. He covered his activities by falsifying reports to head office, while continuing to gamble on futures in the hope of recouping rapidly escalating losses. By December 1994, he had lost the bank more than £200 million and things were about to get a lot worse. The Kobe earthquake on 17 January, 1995, sent shockwaves not just through the landscape of Japan but also through the Nikkei stock exchange and Leeson's losses rocketed.

On 23 February, 1995, Leeson went on the run, catching a plane to Kuala Lumpur with his wife. By now he had run up debts for Barings of £827 million – almost three times the entire reserves of the bank. Realising that the game was up, he booked a flight to London in the hope that any criminal proceedings would take place there, but he was intercepted and arrested in Frankfurt. In November he was extradited to Singapore, where he was sentenced to six-and-a-half years in prison. He was released in 1999. A subsequent Bank of England enquiry blamed 'a failure of management and other internal controls of the most basic kind' for the fact that Leeson's activities had gone undetected with such dire consequences. Barings Bank was eventually bought for £1 by the Dutch banking and insurance giant ING.

ACTING WITH INDISCRETION

David Mellor – seen here in happier days with his first wife at a fete in his Putney constituency on 25 July, 1992 – was one of several Tory MPs with something to hide. Recently appointed secretary of state for national heritage, he became the central figure in a lurid kiss-and-tell scandal involving his mistress, actress Antonia de Sanchez. The tabloid press had a field day with allegations of his penchant for toe-sucking and, according to her account, his preference for making love dressed in a Chelsea football strip. Mellor actually rode out the sex scandal. When he was eventually forced to resign it was over a different allegation that he had accepted air tickets and the use of a villa from Monica Bauwens, the daughter of a leading official in the Palestine Liberation Organisation. When he quit office, *The Sun* exultantly headlined the news 'Toe Job To No Job.'

sought his downfall. Bill Hagerty, the editor of *The People*, the newspaper that led the way in probing into Mellor's conduct, commented simply that his resignation was 'the first time in ages that David Mellor has done the decent thing'.

Scandal followed scandal. Some people laughed, but many more were outraged. In April 1997, following the Prime Minister's ill-advised attempt to rebrand the Conservatives as the party of the family – the 'most important institution in our lives', as Major put it – the *Daily Mirror* responded by printing on its front page photographs of eight Conservative MPs who, as editor Piers Morgan exuberantly reported, had all 'done their bit for the family recently'. The unfortunate eight were identified as 'Mr Toesucker (David Mellor), Mr Randy (Rob Richards), Mr Rampant (Alan Clark), Mr Fiddler (Rupert Allason), Mr Cradle-Snatcher (Piers Merchant), Mr Lovechild (Tim Yeo), Mr Goes-Like-a-Train (Stephen Norris) and Mr Swinger (Jerry Hayes).' Morgan noted in his diary: 'It's a bit childish, but bloody funny. And it signals our intent to get stuck into the Tories big time on their most vulnerable issue – sleaze.'

Arms for Iraq

Sexual shenanigans were bad enough for the government, but there were other more serious issues at stake. A really major scandal concerning the allegedly illegal export of arms systems to Iraq had been rumbling away in the background even before Major came to power. It reached a head in 1991, when three executives of Matrix Churchill, a machine-tool concern based in Coventry, were arrested and charged with deceiving the government as to the intended destination and purpose of the machine-tools they had supplied to Saddam Hussein's murderous regime.

HIGH-PROFILE WHISTLEBLOWER
When his bid to win British citizenship failed, Egyptian businessman Mohammed Al Fayed, the owner of Harrods in Knightsbridge since 1985, determined to expose the sleaze that he insisted permeated Parliament – in particular, he made allegations against certain MPs whom he considered had let him down. He claimed that he had paid Tory MP Neil Hamilton more than £50,000 in cash, plus further sums channelled via Ian Greer Associates, to campaign for him in the House of Commons. In addition, Al Fayed said Hamilton and his wife had stayed free of charge for six nights at the Ritz Hotel in Paris, another of Al Fayed's prestigious acquisitions, where this picture of him was taken in 1995. They did not stint themselves, he complained, drinking vintage champagne every evening. Al Fayed also claimed that he had made payments to Tim Smith to raise questions in Parliament on his behalf. Like Neil Hamilton, Smith was forced to resign from the government.

'I felt it was my public duty to make these facts known.'
Mohammed Al Fayed, on making allegations about MPs Neil Hamilton and Tim Smith

VOTERS TAKE REVENGE

Neil Hamilton and his wife Christine (right), on 8 April, 1997, celebrating his selection as Conservative candidate for Tatton in Cheshire for the forthcoming general election. His local party may have given him the thumbs up, but the voters did not: instead they elected Martin Bell (below), a former war correspondent for the BBC, who stood as an independent anti-sleaze candidate and overthrew Hamilton's 16,000 majority. Hamilton, who had been MP for the constituency since 1983, and his one-time associate Ian Greer sued *The Guardian* for printing 'cash-for-questions' allegations made by Mohammed Al Fayed. They dropped the case when it emerged that Hamilton had been paid a retainer by Greer's PR company which the MP had failed to declare. A subsequent enquiry by Sir Gordon Downey, the Commissioner for Parliamentary Standards, reported in July 1977 that there was 'compelling evidence' to suggest that Hamilton had indeed pocketed Al Fayed cash.

'My primary concern in fighting this case is to clear my name, but I am also determined to remove the slur the cash-for-questions case has cast over Parliament as a whole.'

Neil Hamilton, in 1996, before withdrawing his libel suit against *The Guardian*

The trial of the Matrix-Churchill executives, which opened the following year, went badly for the government from the start. Attempts to withhold critical documents from the defence by issuing so-called Public Interest Immunity Certificates failed when the judge trying the case ordered the documents to be supplied. There was every suspicion that the truth was being covered up, especially when the defendants claimed that at least some ministers had known what they were doing right from the start. The case against the men collapsed completely when Alan Clark, who had been Minister for Trade at the time, admitted in the witness-box that the notes of a crucial Department of Trade meeting had been 'economical' with the truth and that he was fully aware the machine tools in question could be used to manufacture munitions.

The resulting outcry was such that Lord Justice Scott was hastily appointed to head an official enquiry into the case. His report, published three years later, was a devastating exposé of the workings of the Whitehall machine. Scott found that the government had failed to disclose to Parliament its decision to adopt a more liberal attitude to defence sales to Iraq. He singled out Sir Nicholas Lyell, the Attorney-General, and William Waldegrave, Chief Secretary of the Treasury, for specific criticism. To the man-in-the-street, the whole episode wreaked of duplicity and double dealing. The Bishop of Ely reflected the feelings of most ordinary folk when he said scathingly that the report provided 'evidence of an obsession with secrecy, disregard for the truth and a willingness to mislead Parliament'.

'Cash for questions'

It was yet another blow to the government's fast-fading reputation – another was to follow. In October 1994 Mohamed Al Fayed, the controversial owner of Harrods, revealed to *The Guardian* that he had paid two high-flying Tory MPs £2,000 a time to ask parliamentary questions on his behalf. The newspaper article claimed that both men had received pay-offs in wads of £50 notes, neatly stuffed into brown envelopes. Tim Smith, one of the MPs named by Al Fayed, was now a junior Northern Ireland minister. The flamboyant Neil Hamilton, a junior minister at the Department of Trade and Industry, was the other; in one of those curious ironies, Hamilton's job included special responsibility for business probity.

In Hamilton's case, Al Fayed had more allegations to make public. Telling the press that he 'felt it was my public duty to make these facts known', he went on to describe how, at Hamilton's request, he had arranged for the MP and his wife to stay at the Ritz Hotel in Paris for a week. In addition to waiving payment for their hotel stay, he had picked up a £2,000 bill for extras, including their bar bill and the cost of hiring a car. He had also allowed them to shop for free at Harrods.

Smith quickly admitted his guilt and resigned, but Hamilton, though obliged to quit as Corporate Affairs Minister, protested his innocence and fought on. Together with Ian Greer, the head of the PR firm that, it was alleged, had channelled Al Fayed's payments to Hamilton, he sued the newspaper for libel. A day before the case was due to start both men, who had by this time fallen out, dropped their action, saying that they could not afford to continue. The next day, *The Guardian* celebrated with a front-page picture of Hamilton beneath a headline reading simply 'A Liar and A Cheat.'

And so to jail

Hamilton was not the only one of Major's ministers to look to the courts for redress. The swashbuckling Jonathan Aitken, Minister for Defence Procurement and then Chief Secretary to the Treasury, was another. He sued both *The Guardian* and the TV current affairs programme *World in Action* for alleging that he had personally profited from brokering British arms sales to Saudi Arabia. He resigned from the Cabinet in order to pursue the case, saying that it had fallen to him 'to start a fight to cut out the cancer of bent and twisted journalism in our country with the simple sword of truth and the trusty shield of British fair play'.

It took until June 1997 for the case to get to court. It collapsed when George Carman, counsel for both *The Guardian* and *World in Action*, produced documentary evidence to prove that Aitken had lied under oath when he said that his wife had paid the hotel bill for a crucial weekend stay in Paris. In fact, she had not even been there at the time – she had been in Switzerland and the bill had been picked up by Aitken's Arab associate.

Aitken was ruined politically and financially. So, too, was Neil Hamilton. Both men had lost their seats in the general election held in May. But then, so had many other Conservative MPs who were not guilty of sleaze or wasting the court's time. The Major years were over. An optimistic nation waited expectantly to see what the Blair ones would bring.

FROM CABINET TO PRISON CELL
Disgraced minister Jonathan Aitken at the 1995 Conservative Party conference, before his fall from grace. Here again, it was a revelation by Mohammed Al Fayed that would turn out to have serious repercussions for a high-flying Tory MP. It was alleged that during Aitken's tenure as Minister of Defence Procurement he had stayed at the Ritz hotel in Paris and the bill had been paid by a Saudi Arabian arms dealer. Aitken, now promoted to a member of the Cabinet, indignantly declared his innocence and resigned his post as Chief Secretary to the Treasury to take on his accusers in court. The move backfired in spectacular fashion when Aitken's version of events was shown to be untrue and the case collapsed. He was subsequently tried for perjury and perverting the course of justice and in 1999 went to prison, serving seven months of an 18-month sentence.

POWER TRAIN

Tony and Cherie Blair chat with an attentive Sir Richard Branson on board one of Branson's Virgin trains in April 1997, during the general election campaign. Blair won by a landslide to become Prime Minister on 1 May, just short of his 43rd birthday. Voting showed a 10.9 per cent swing to Labour, which gave them 418 seats in the House of Commons compared to the Conservatives' 165 and the Liberals' 46. The Scots and Welsh Nationalists netted 10 seats between them. Blair fought the campaign with carefully calculated sound bites and sometimes windy rhetoric that was notably light on spelling out the details of actual policies or the ways in which they would be implemented. What was concealed by Blair's affable manner and friendly exterior was the ruthless way in which he and his fellow modernisers had transformed Old Labour into New Labour. The days of the block vote and the trade union barons were over. Once in power, it swiftly became clear that the determination of policy would be left firmly in the hands of Blair and a close circle of friends and advisers.

A NEW BEGINNING

Most Britons were expecting New Labour to win the May 1997 general election, but the immensity of the triumph took even Tony Blair by surprise. Before the early results were declared, Blair confided to close colleagues that he would be satisfied with a 30 to 40-seat advantage over the Conservatives. In the event, Labour came to power with an overall majority of 179 seats – 33 more than Clement Attlee had won back in the post-war Labour landslide of 1945. The humiliated Conservatives had their worst result since 1906, clinging on in just 165 constituencies. They lost more than 60 seats in and around London, and finished election night with no seats at all in Birmingham, Liverpool, Manchester, Leeds or Sheffield. There was not a single Tory MP in the whole of Scotland and Wales.

THE PEOPLE'S CHOICE Tony and Cherie Blair make their way into Downing Street on a tide of goodwill after Labour's landslide victory in the May 1997 election. Blair was the first Labour Prime Minister since James Callaghan in 1979.

NEW LABOUR TAKES POWER

It was the landslide to end all landslides. Tony Blair was heard to mutter 'it can't be real', shaking his head in disbelief as leading Tories were skittled out like ninepins. David Mellor and Norman Lamont lost in Putney and Kingston-upon-Thames, while Malcolm Rifkind, the former Foreign Secretary, lost his seat at Pentlands. Perhaps the shock of the night came when Michael Portillo, former Defence Secretary and darling of the Tory right, was ousted at Enfield. Piers Morgan, editor of the *Daily Mirror*, recorded how 'a huge cheer went up in the Mirror newsroom' when Portillo fell. Soon afterwards, the ebullient Morgan made his way to the Royal Festival Hall, where thousands of New Labour stalwarts were celebrating to the strains of the pop song 'Things Can Only Get Better', the party's anthem for the campaign. It was, some claimed, a new dawn for Britain.

There was no doubting the new Prime Minister's personal popularity. He was the youngest man to become premier in the 20th century. John Major announced his intention to resign the Conservative leadership as soon as his shattered party could choose a successor. 'When the curtain falls', he declared, 'it's time to get off the stage and that's what I propose to do.'

OUT WITH THE OLD, IN WITH THE NEW
A horde of press photographers, reporters and TV cameramen wait for Tony Blair to enter Downing Street in triumph and take his place in No.10 for the first time as Prime Minister. The defeated John Major was already on his way out; here (left), his portrait is being packed away, ready for despatch to his home, together with his personal papers and other possessions. New Labour had won 418 seats in the House of Commons, leaving the Conservatives with just 165, the Liberal Democrats 46 and 28 shared among the other parties. Major easily kept his own seat in Huntingdon, but some of his leading colleagues – Michael Portillo and Malcolm Rifkind among them – were not so fortunate. By all measures, it was a truly historic victory for Labour.

'Today's politics is about the search for security in a changing world. We must build the strong and active society that will provide it.'

Tony Blair, Labour Party Conference, 1994

UNITED IN VICTORY
Tony Blair and John Prescott stand to applaud Chancellor Gordon Brown's keynote speech to the post-election party conference in Brighton in 1997. Brown swiftly won a reputation for fiscal prudence which made him a favourite of the City of London. One of his first decisions was to shift responsibility for setting interest rates from the Treasury to the Bank of England.

THE RISE OF NEW LABOUR

Tony Blair christened it 'the Project'. Its aim was to transform the old Labour Party into a modern political machine that could take control of the middle ground in politics. The campaign started in 1994, following the death of John Smith, when Blair won the party leadership polling 57 per cent of the vote. Gordon Brown, the shadow chancellor, was the other major player in the modernisation project. Key members of what was dubbed 'Team Tony' included Peter Mandelson, Alastair Campbell (who ran Blair's press office), pollster Philip Gould, Derry Irvine (who would become Blair's Lord Chancellor) and Anji Hunter, a political fixer *par excellence*. Between them, they masterminded the transformation process that was to turn Old Labour into New Labour once and for all.

BACKROOM BUDDIES
Alastair Campbell, whom Blair appointed as Downing Street's Director of Communications after taking power, chats to Cherie Blair on one of the many train journeys made in the course of the 1997 election campaign. Relations between Campbell and Cherie were not always as cordial as they appear to be here. Cherie, a prominent civil rights barrister who had risen to be appointed Queen's Counsel, was determined to be her own woman in Downing Street and resisted attempts to keep her 'on message' toeing the official government line. Campbell became exasperated by her sometimes controversial interventions, which increased in frequency as time went by.

CHIPS ON THE STUMP

John Prescott and Shona McIsaac, the Labour candidate for Cleethorpes, pause for fish and chips during a constituency walkabout in 1996. Following Labour's election victory, Prescott was promoted from Deputy Leader of the Labour Party to Deputy Prime Minister. Initially, he was also given a Cabinet portfolio as Secretary of State for the Environment, Transport and the Regions. As a former ship's steward and trade union activist, Prescott was uniquely placed to provide the essential link for Tony Blair and the other middle class New Labour modernisers with the Party's traditional working-class supporters and activists. Later, another of his tasks was to try to keep the peace between Prime Minister and Chancellor as the relationship between the two men became more and more strained.

TRY TO SEE IT MY WAY

Gordon Brown voices his opinion to Peter Mandelson, Alastair Campbell, Tony Blair and Margaret Beckett during the 1997 election campaign. All of them were determined that this time Labour would not squander its chance of regaining power, which was why the manifesto they devised contained so few specific pledges. Blair largely confined himself to generalities. 'I want a Britain that is one nation with shared values and purposes, where merit comes before privilege, run for the many not the few, strong and sure of itself at home and abroad', he wrote. Worthy aims perhaps, but he gave little actual indication of how these goals would be achieved. Two specific pledges made by New Labour were negative rather than positive. Blair and Brown promised not to raise income tax and to abide by the spending limits set by the previous Tory government for two years.

BLAIR'S BABES
Two days after his election triumph, Tony Blair poses with some of the 101 Labour women MPs. Nearly one in four of Labour's new MPs were women and the overall total dwarfed previous records for numbers of women elected. Some were astonished to be there. Clare Curtis-Thomas, newly elected MP for Crosby, later recalled: 'I was in a state of shock … I'd been told my seat was unwinnable. When the results came out, I burst into tears.' A few rose to high office, but others became disillusioned with the whole political process. Tess Kingham, MP for Gloucester, decided to stand down at the next general election, bitterly criticising the 'public school atmosphere and outdated practices' of Parliament.

New Labour had worked flat out for their victory. Piers Morgan later recalled how he was personally conducted around the aptly named war rooms in the party's Millbank headquarters by Gordon Brown, now Chancellor designate, and Peter Mandelson, the master of spin who, many believed, had been instrumental in propelling Blair to the top of the political tree. 'It was a stunningly efficient and impressive set-up, a bit like a political NASA centre', he wrote. 'It's a ruthless machine, with the latest technology to support it.'

Cloth caps and donkey jackets were out. Smart business suits were in. So, too, were pledge cards and focus groups. Off-the-cuff comments were banned as pagers made sure that everyone stayed 'on message.' Blair and Brown assiduously wooed the business community – especially the financiers of the City of London. They pledged that there would be no rises in direct taxation for top earners when they came to power and that they would stick to the public spending limits set by the Conservatives. New Labour, Blair said, would be 'wise spenders, not big spenders'. It would be economically capable, fiscally prudent and a champion of opportunity, wealth creation and individual aspiration. It shared the hopes and ambitions of the once derided middle classes. In a rare unguarded moment Peter Mandelson summed up the new attitude when he remarked that he was 'intensely relaxed about people getting filthy rich'.

Blair benefited, too, from the support of practically the entire press, in particular that of Australian media mogul Rupert Murdoch and the *Sun*. Back in 1992, the morning after John Major's surprise election victory over Neil Kinnock, the *Sun*'s headline had proudly proclaimed 'It Was The Sun Wot Won It'. Tony Blair was not going to risk the same happening again. In 1995 he flew to Australia to deliver the keynote speech at a News International conference presided over by Murdoch and won the all-important backing of his leading British tabloid. It was the end of more than 20 years of *Sun* support for the Tories. This time round it told its readers the Tories were 'tired, divided and rudderless'. Its support for Blair was unswerving. 'The people need a leader with vision, purpose and courage who can inspire them and fire their imagination,' the paper declared. 'The *Sun* believes that man is Tony Blair!'

Building a new Britain

New Labour's election manifesto may have been short on specifics, but with more than 200 pledges it certainly promised a lot. Blair called for better schools, better hospitals and new ways of tackling crime. A New Labour government, he said, would modernise the welfare state while enabling the country to thrive in what he called a revolutionary new world economy. 'I want', wrote Blair, 'a society where we do not simply pursue our own individual aims, but where we hold many aims in common and work together to achieve them.' He went on to set out the key priorities that he and his government were determined to tackle first.

BATTLING FOR PEACE
Mo Mowlam, the Secretary of State for Northern Ireland, arrives in Downing Street to join Tony Blair in the talks with Nationalist and Loyalist leaders that would culminate in the Good Friday Agreement. Mowlam was a much-respected politician and instrumental in that agreement being reached, but her willingness to speak her mind did not always go down well. Loyalist leader David Trimble eventually demanded that she be sacked, complaining that she was too sympathetic to Sinn Fein. 'One of the great difficulties we have had', he said, 'has been the widespread lack of confidence in the community, particularly among Ulster Unionists, with regard to what the Secretary of State will do.'

'It was not pessimists and reactionaries who built Britain's greatness, but visionaries, optimists and idealists.'

Gordon Brown

GIRL POWER
The Spice Girls – left to right, Melanie Chisholm (Sporty Spice), Gerri Haliwell (Ginger), Emma Bunton (Baby), Melanie Brown (Scary) and Victoria Adams (Posh) – joke with the Prince of Wales at a gala performance to mark the 21st anniversary of the Prince's Trust at the Manchester Opera House in 1997. Though they were chart-topping megastars, this was the first time the girls had sung live as a band. They were clearly not intimidated by the occasion. Scary Spice and Ginger Spice both kissed Prince Charles on the cheek, with Ginger telling him that he was 'very sexy'. The Prince and his two young sons were fans. When Geri Halliwell finally quit the band, he wrote to her to say that 'the group will not be the same without you'. Posh Spice would remain in the media spotlight following her marriage to footballing star David Beckham.

The National Health Service was to be reinvigorated and reformed. More was to be done to get the unemployed – particularly the young – off benefits and into work. Blair also made dealing with crime a priority. New Labour, he promised, would be 'tough on crime and tough on the causes of crime', notably by introducing a fast-track punishment scheme for persistent young offenders. Continuing a trend set by the Tories, there would be 'zero tolerance' of street beggars and other social victims.

Top of Blair's priority list was education. Class sizes, he promised, would be reduced, standards in schools improved and nursery places provided for all four-year-olds. Recognising that personal computers were becoming an integral part of everyday life, he pledged that all schoolchildren would be guaranteed access to a computer terminal and to the Internet and they would all be given individual email addresses (in the event, this last promise went unfulfilled). The emphasis on information technology was apposite for Sir Tim Berners-Lees, inventor of the World Wide Web, was British. By the time Blair came to power, everyone who had Internet access was surfing the Web. Emails were equally ubiquitous, while mobile telephones, which had been growing smaller over the years, now slipped handily into most people's pockets. It was a new world for Britain.

Un-Labour-like ways

It was what most people wanted to hear, but on closer examination it seemed to some that there was relatively little substance behind the flim-flam. In some ways, too, Tony Blair – who had gone on record as being something of an admirer of Margaret Thatcher – turned out to be as conservative as the Conservatives. Rather than being repealed, for instance, existing Tory legislation controlling the power of trade unions remained in force. Privatisation continued to gain pace, though Blair and Brown together did their best to dress it up as what they called the Private Finance Initiative, a so-called fiscal partnership between the state and private sectors of the economy.

Above all, Gordon Brown claimed to be fiscally prudent, the New Labour publicity machine hailing him as the 'Iron Chancellor.' There were the beginnings of rumblings, though, when what were soon labelled 'stealth taxes' started to be imposed. True to New Labour's manifesto promise, Brown did not put up income tax, but the tax thresholds were frozen so an extra 1.5 million people found themselves paying tax at the top rate. Costs were shuffled from national to local government with the consequence that council tax began to rise. What proved to be the most controversial move of all was the Chancellor's decision to abolish tax concessions on share dividends. Though Brown said that this was simply a sensible technical reform, it cost the private pension funds dearly. Members of such schemes eventually found themselves worse off by a staggering £100 billion.

As the country emerged from recession and started to prosper once more, unemployment began to fall, but the old notion of 'a job for life' was fast disappearing. Instead, in what the pundits termed a 'flexible labour market,' more people found themselves accepting relatively short-term contracts, job-sharing or working part-time. A national minimum wage was introduced, but it was set fairly low at £3.60 an hour. The guaranteed rate for young people, aged between 18 and 21, was even lower at £3.00 per hour. Most controversial of all, university students found themselves being charged tuition fees for the first time in British history. Traditional student maintenance grants were abolished into the bargain.

COOL BRITANNIA

Nothing he did or did not do politically was capable of denting Blair's popularity. Young, active and full of charisma, he seemed to embody the spirit of what had been dubbed 'Cool Britannia'. One of his early acts in Downing Street was to throw a lavish, celebrity-packed party to celebrate British achievement across the cultural scene. British rock and pop music was booming, thanks to bands such as Oasis, Blur, Pulp, Suede, Supergrass, The Verve and the ubiquitous Spice Girls.

POP IDOLS
Blur's lead singer Damon Albarn and bass-player Alex James strut their stuff on stage at the 1998 Glastonbury Festival (left). Together with Oasis, Blur was one of the iconic bands of the 1990s; the supposed public rivalry between the two was hyped as 'the battle of Britpop'. Jarvis Cocker – seen here (right) lighting Liam Gallagher's cigarette at a fund-raising dinner for the charity War Child – was the founder and creative force of Pulp, another leading band of the decade. Liam was one of two Gallagher brothers in Oasis, the other being Noel, and was the more controversial of the two, notorious for drunken outbursts and erratic behaviour both on and off stage. The relationship between Noel and Liam was frequently fraught – at one time, they only spoke to each other on stage.

'Off to the Cool Britannia party at No.10. After all the hype, it was a rather motley gathering of media luvvies, actors and pop stars – all wondering what on earth they were doing there.'

Piers Morgan, *Diaries*

Contemporary British art was on the up as well, with artists such as Sam Taylor-Wood, Damien Hirst and Tracey Emin. British fashion designers – most notably John Galliano and Alexander McQueen – were in demand, as were fashion models. London, proclaimed the magazine *Vanity Fair*, was swinging again. *Newsweek* agreed, reporting that 'hot fashion, a pulsating club scene and lots of new money' was making London 'the coolest city on the planet'.

For many – especially the young – it seemed that Britain had become a different place, or at least felt like it had. Eddie Tyrell, then a Liverpool schoolboy, recollected how 'growing up in the 1990s was fantastic, it seemed anything was possible. Britain was cool again, we had our own music, our own art, our own identity.' Birmingham disc jockey Daniel Kings expressed similar sentiments: 'It was a time,' he recalled, 'when anything seemed possible, a new world order had arrived and the soundtrack was house, techno and drum and bass!'

Teflon Tony

Blair presided over it all with flamboyant equanimity. His popularity never waned, not even when – just six months after coming to power – he was accused of improperly intervening behind the scenes to exempt Formula One motor racing

SUPERMODELS
Kate Moss having her hair fixed before her appearance at London Fashion Week in 1999 (above). At the same event two years earlier, Naomi Campbell strutted down the catwalk modelling a Union Jack top teamed with a blue skirt and red shoes (right). Both Moss and Campbell were born in south London – Moss in Croydon, Campbell in Streatham. Following their rise to the very top of the modelling tree, they both hit the headlines for their at-times wild behaviour. Campbell's reported temper tantrums led her, in 1999, to seek anger management counselling at a celebrity American health clinic. Moss was first spotted, aged only 14, by an agency talent scout as she passed through JFK airport in New York. She made the so-called 'waif look' famous.

from his government's proposed ban
on tobacco advertising in sport. Blair
even admitted in a TV interview that
he had met privately with Bernie
Ecclestone, Formula One's billionaire
boss who some months before had
donated £1 million to New Labour,
but he simply assured the watching
millions that he was 'a pretty straight
sort of guy' and that he 'would never,
ever do something wrong or improper
or change a policy because someone
supported or donated money to the
party'. And viewers believed him. The
party gave Ecclestone his money back.

One of Blair's closest New Labour
colleagues was not so fortunate. Peter
Mandelson was forced out of office
when it was revealed that he had
bought a fashionable home in trendy
Notting Hill with the assistance of a
£373,000 personal loan from Geoffrey
Robinson, the millionaire Paymaster-
General. Not only had Mandelson
failed to declare the loan in the House
of Commons Register of Interests, he
also failed to mention it to his building
society when he took out a mortgage to
raise the rest of the money he needed.
Even more crucially, Robinson's
business dealings were under
investigation by the Department for
Trade and Industry, which Mandelson
headed as Secretary of State.

In the election build-up, Blair had
promised the voters that his
administration, as opposed to that of
the Conservatives, would be 'whiter
than white'. Mandelson had to go.
Insisting to the end that, though he
might have been 'technically wrong' in
not telling his building society about
the loan, he had done nothing
improper, Mandelson resigned.
Robinson followed him, while Charlie
Whelan, Gordon Brown's controversial
press secretary, was also forced to quit,
suspected of leaking the story of the
loan to the press.

BUT IS IT ART?

Damien Hirst (left), the *enfant terrible* of British art in the 1990s, poses for the camera in the days before he gave up drinking and smoking. The waiter looks less than impressed. Hirst's approach to his art – and the work that he produced as a result – was never less than unconventional, but he nevertheless made a fortune from it, as did others. In his lengthily titled piece 'The Physical Impossibility of Death in the Mind of Someone Living', he displayed a dead 14-foot tiger shark preserved in a tank filled with formaldehyde. The piece had been commissioned by advertising guru and modern art collector Charles Saatchi, who eventually sold it for $8 million, a sum that previously would have been thought high even for an Old Master. For some, it was a symbol of the BritArt Renaissance; but for others, a dead shark was simply not art at all.

By contrast David Hockney, seen here (right) in trademark white cap at a 1997 exhibition, enjoyed unreserved success, praise and respect as an artist. He is universally hailed as the doyen of modern British Pop Art.

'I just wanted to find out where the boundaries were. I've found there aren't any. I wanted to be stopped but no one will stop me.'

Damien Hirst

HEIGHT OF FASHION

STUNNINGLY ORIGINAL
British fashion designers were not afraid of being outrageous. Vivienne Westwood, seen here (left) embracing supermodel Naomi Campbell at the 1993 Designer of the Year awards, had started the punk revolution back in the 1970s. In the 1990s, she still had the power to shock with controversial catwalk shows.

Alexander McQueen's clothes stood out for their beautiful tailoring, as in this deftly embroidered bodice from 1996 (below left). McQueen had the generous support of magazine editor and fashion icon Isabella Blow (below centre); she was one of the first to recognise his talents, purchasing his entire graduation collection. The colourful coat (below right) was created by John Galliano in 1998 for Christian Dior, inspired by indigenous South American art.

In Cool Britannia, clothes designers, together with rock stars, avant-garde film-makers and trendy architects, were among the new social elite. British fashion designers such as Vivienne Westwood were taking centre stage on the world's catwalks. John Galliano, who began his career in London, won universal recognition as one of the most exciting, innovative and visionary designers of the day; *Time* magazine hailed him as 'the most influential fashion designer of his generation'. His controversial contemporary Alexander McQueen was just as successful.

'Clothes and jewellery should be startling, individual. When you see a woman in my clothes, you want to know more about them. To me, that is what distinguishes good designers from bad designers.'

Alexander McQueen

THE WORLD OF FASHIONISTAS
The fashion world of the 1990s was full of colourful characters. Menswear icon Paul Smith (opposite, top left) originally won fame for his idiosyncratic take on traditional British men's styling. It was, he wrote, 'classic with a twist'. Later, he branched out into clothes for women as well. Irish milliner Philip Treacy – seen here taking applause in 1997 amidst a group of models all wearing his fabulous hats (opposite, bottom) – was another highly individual designer. Fashionista Isabella Blow helped him to break into the world of high fashion, but even as a student he had been hailed in the *Sunday Times* by Claire Stubbs, then fashion director of Harrods, as 'the next great British hat-maker'. In his designs, Treacy aimed to create something novel and instantly eye-catching, yet at the same time comfortable to wear. 'I hate rules and formulas', he said. 'That's so boring. It's the opposite of creativity. Rules are ridiculous things that are made to be broken.' Alexander McQueen (opposite, top right) and John Galliano (left) were just as innovative and unconventional. They both began their careers in London, but were quickly snapped up by Paris fashion houses. The photograph of McQueen with the falcon was taken at the end of Givenchy's high-fashion collection launch in 1997.

The Nineties was also the age of supermodels, jetting around the world from catwalk to catwalk and making fortunes in the process. Kate Moss and Jodie Kidd – seen here (above) flanking Stella McCartney, daughter of Paul, who became one of the decade's rising fashion-design stars – were typical of the new waif-like breed, but it was Canadian model Linda Evangelista who summed up what many took to be the typical supermodel attitude. In 1990, she jokingly told *Vogue*: 'We don't wake up for less than $10,000 a day.'

DIANA – QUEEN OF HEARTS

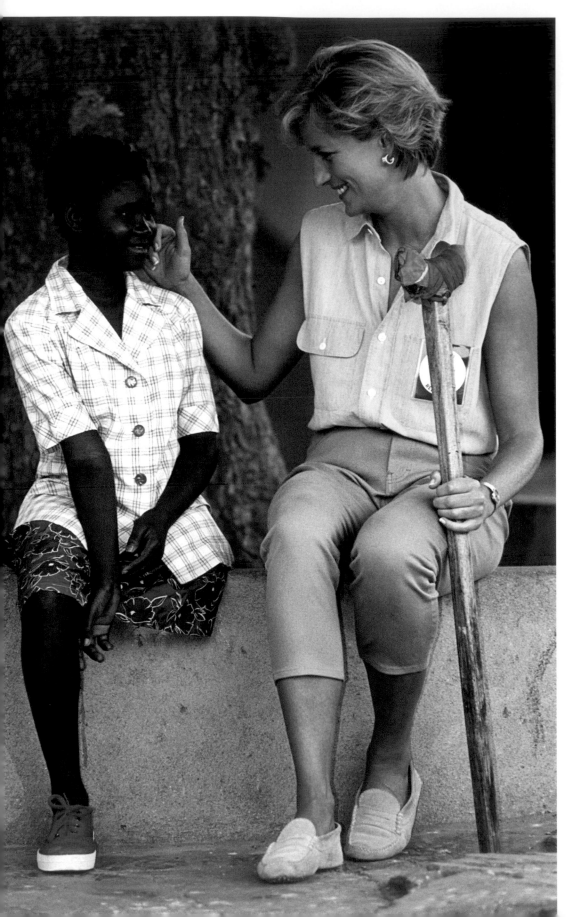

As Blair's opinion poll ratings remained sky-high, there was only one figure who could constantly outshine him – Diana, Princess of Wales. Divorce from Prince Charles, finalised in July 1996, had done nothing to dim her appeal. She had become a celebrity icon, a charismatic, shining super-star, without rival on the global stage.

Some might have held that, by behaving more like a movie heroine or pop diva than a traditional princess, Diana was cheapening the institution of monarchy, but the vast majority of the British public begged to differ. They had taken her to their hearts like no other royal figure before or since, and the way that she behaved was all part and parcel of the attraction. She captivated the public imagination partly through force of personality and partly by astute handling of the media to her advantage. Over and above her undoubted elegance and beauty, she displayed a personal vulnerability that ordinary people could relate to. 'There were three in this marriage', she told BBC reporter Martin Bashir, 'so it was a bit crowded.' Her sensational interview shown on *Panorama* in November 1995 was watched by millions, who felt her sadness, hurt and pain.

Despite all his attempts to tell his side of the story, the Prince of Wales stood no chance of deflecting the copious public criticism that came his way. Nor was there the remotest possibility that Diana would go quietly, as all the senior members of the royal family clearly would have liked. Quite apart from being mother to William and Harry, second and third in line to the throne, she believed that she still had an important role to play, whether

COMPASSION
Diana, Princess of Wales, meets a young
girls from Angola, the victim of a landmine,
in Luanda for treatment at an orthopaedic
workshop in 1997. The Princess flew to
Africa to see for herself what damage these
lethal anti-personnel weapons were causing
and returned determined to press for an
international ban on their use. 'The mine',
she said, 'is a stealthy killer. Long after
conflict is ended, its innocent victims die or
are wounded singly in countries of which
we hear little.' Pictures of her walking
through a minefield wearing a protective
helmet and flak jacket were beamed around
the world. The Princess got her way. Later
that year, delegates from 88 nations met in
Oslo to draw up the terms of a treaty
banning the production, stockpiling and
use of landmines.

it was counselling sufferers from depression and eating disorders, kissing and comforting AIDS patients and cancer victims, or campaigning against the use of landmines. 'I think', she said in the same *Panorama* interview, 'the British people need someone in public life to give affection, to make them feel important, to support them, to give them light in their dark tunnels.' As she was no longer going to become the actual Queen, she would, she said, simply 'like to be a Queen of people's hearts, in people's hearts.'

Tragedy in Paris

What Diana would or would not do was the talk of the nation in the long, hot summer of 1997. That July, having recently begun a new friendship with Dodi Al Fayed, eldest son of the multi-millionaire owner of Harrods, she departed for a brief holiday at the luxurious Al Fayed villa in the south of France, accompanied by her two schoolboy sons, William and Harry. 'I will shock you with what I am going to do next', she told the pack of reporters and photographers – the infamous paparazzi – who pursued her onto the beaches.

A week or so later, it became clear what she meant. Rumours began to percolate through Fleet Street that she and Dodi were fast becoming more than just friends. They were an item. On 8 August, the *Sunday Mirror* broke the news, splashing a picture across its front page of the world's hottest couple kissing in the sea. The headline read simply 'The Kiss'.

It was a story that warmed most people's hearts, but tragedy swiftly followed. In the early hours of 31 August, Diana, Dodi and their driver all died as the result of a car crash, when their speeding car hit a pillar and smashed into a wall in an underpass in Paris. The driver had been trying to shake off pursuing paparazzi. Dodi died on the scene. Diana was cut from the wreckage and rushed to hospital, where a team of surgeons struggled to save her. They failed. At 4.00am, Diana, Princess of Wales, was officially pronounced dead.

CONFESSION
The Princess showed herself to be a natural
on TV when, in November 1995, shortly
after her separation from Prince Charles,
she appeared on *Panorama* in an hour-long
special interview with Martin Bashir. Millions
across the nation sat riveted as she opened
her heart. Breaking every royal taboo, she
spoke freely about the strain of being a
member of the royal family, her depression
and bulimia, her husband's lack of
compassion towards her and his on-going
relationship with Camilla Parker Bowles.
She was equally frank about her own
relationships, admitting that she had
conducted an adulterous affair with her
riding instructor, Captain James Hewitt.

SEA OF FLOWERS
A lone policewoman casts an early morning shadow across the bouquets of flowers covering the approach to Kensington Palace, Diana's former home. It was just two days after the Princess's tragic death in a high-speed car crash in Paris. The detail (left) shows the ironwork of the palace gates, decorated with flowers and a photograph of the Princess. In an unprecedented reaction, people poured into the capital in their thousands, from all over the country and abroad, to pay their last respects to the 'Queen of Hearts'. By the end of the week, it was estimated that a million floral tributes had been reverently laid outside Kensington Palace, Buckingham Palace and St James's Palace, where the Princess's body lay in state.

The 'People's Princess'

The Prime Minister was one of the first to get the news. He then spoke to the Queen, herself on holiday at Balmoral with Prince Charles and the two young princes. She told him that neither she nor any other member of the royal family would be making an official statement.

But Blair quickly realised that something had to be said. Standing outside his local church later that morning, he spoke for the nation. 'I feel, like everyone else in this country today, utterly devastated', he began, continuing with a moving tribute to Diana's 'compassion and humanity'. He concluded resonantly: 'People everywhere, not just here in Britain, kept faith with Princess Diana. They liked her, they loved her, they regarded her as one of the people. She was the People's Princess and that is how she will stay, how she will remain in our hearts and our memories forever.'

A nation in mourning

The premier had captured the public mood perfectly. No sooner had the news of Diana's death broken than people of all ages, from all walks of life, began pouring into London at an estimated rate of around 6,000 an hour. Before long, the gates of Kensington Palace, her London home, and surrounding streets and pavements were festooned with flowers, teddy bears, Queen of Hearts playing cards, rosaries and children's drawings. People camped out waiting to pay their respects – there were lines of sleeping bags stretching the length of Pall Mall. Many erected makeshift shrines with candles burning in front of pictures of the princess. Strangers hugged strangers. People wept openly in the streets. The capital had never seen anything quite like it.

Everyone was waiting for some gesture from the royal family. None came. Public incredulity at what was perceived as callousness swiftly turned to anger. Rumours abounded, one of which had it that the Queen favoured a private interment, rather than a lavish state funeral that people felt Diana more than deserved. What everyone forgot was that Diana, now divorced, was no longer a member of the royal family and the funeral was not the Queen's to decide.

GRANDSONS AND GRANDMOTHER
Prince William and Prince Harry outside Westminster Abbey during their mother's funeral; the Queen is pictured walking among the crowds at St James's Palace on her return from Scotland two days before the event. Initially, senior royals – with the exception of the Prince of Wales, who knew more than anyone how far Diana had captured the public's affections – totally misread the public mood. The Queen decided to stay put in Balmoral to comfort and protect the two young princes. She also favoured a quiet private funeral. The public was having none of this. As the protests at apparent royal indifference swelled, a lavish state funeral was hastily organised. Author and playwright John Mortimer summed the situation up quite accurately in the *Evening Standard*: 'This is a ceremony created by the people, a day when principles of protocol are falling like ninepins.'

Then there was the question of why a flag was not flying at half-mast over Buckingham Palace. In vain did traditionalists point out that the flag was lowered only following the death of a sovereign and that, in any case, the Royal Standard was flown only when the Queen herself was in residence. Such answers satisfied no-one. Nor were people happy at the Queen's apparent reluctance to return to London. The popular newspapers – themselves under heavy criticism for their blatant encouragement of the paparazzi whose activities, many believed, had contributed directly to the tragic accident – were quick to join in the calls for a royal show of grief. 'Show Us You Care', the *Daily Express* demanded. The *Daily Mirror* pleaded 'Your People Are Suffering, Speak To Us Ma'am.' The *Daily Mail* was blunt: 'Has The House Of Windsor A Heart?'.

Even the Queen's popularity, never before in doubt, came into question. Just in time, the royal family changed tack. The Queen returned to London and addressed the nation on television, while plans were set in motion for the staging of a lavish state funeral. Prince Charles had already flown to Paris to collect his former wife's body and bring her back to Britain for burial. The service was to take place in Westminster Abbey, after which Diana's funeral procession would progress north through the streets of the capital to the M1 motorway and on to Althorp, her family home. The Spencer family had singled out a small island on a lake in the grounds for the private interment. It swiftly became an unofficial national shrine.

'Goodbye, England's Rose'

On 6 September – a Saturday – Britain said farewell to Princess Diana at the end of an unprecedented week of national mourning. Thousands had queued for days to sign the book of condolence at St James's Palace. Now, the country came to a standstill. More than a million people lined the route that the coffin would take from Kensington Palace to the Abbey and then, after the service, to Northamptonshire. The funeral cortege was four miles long. At its head, walking just behind the gun-carriage bearing the coffin, were the Prince of Wales, the two young Princes, the Duke of Edinburgh and Earl Spencer, Diana's brother. Many in the crowd wept as the coffin passed. Some applauded quietly, while others showered the gun-carriage with flowers. Most simply stood in silent prayer.

Inside the Abbey, charity workers, doctors and nurses, pop and rock musicians, Hollywood stars such as Tom Hanks, Nicole Kidman and Tom Cruise, TV personalities, top fashion designers, politicians and all those others who had received invitations stood almost cheek to cheek. The editors of tabloid newspapers had been excluded at the personal request of Diana's grieving mother.

The Archbishop of Canterbury conducted the service. Both Diana's sisters delivered tributes, while the Prime Minister, who had liked and done his best to help the Princess, read the lesson. Elton John performed a hastily rewritten version of 'Candle in the Wind', a song originally written as a lament for Marilyn Monroe, another public icon who like Diana had tragically died at the age of 36. Earl Spencer delivered the final, controversial, address. He described Diana as the 'very essence of compassion, of duty, of style, of beauty' before blaming the media for causing her death. She was, he said, 'the most hunted person of the modern age'.

There was more to come. Pledging that the young Princes' 'blood family' would do all that they could to guide them as their dead mother would have wished, the Earl launched a barely veiled attack on the royal family for the way they had treated his sister. She 'needed no royal title to generate her particular brand of magic', he said in reference to the decision to deprive Diana of her title 'Her Royal Highness' after her divorce. As he spoke, the crowd outside started to clap and even some of the congregation applauded. The Queen sat with head bowed, listening intently, but not displaying a flicker of emotion. Earl Spencer concluded by giving thanks for 'the life of a woman I am so proud to be able to call my sister – the unique, the complex, the extraordinary and irreplaceable Diana, whose beauty, both internal and external, will never be extinguished from our minds.'

It was an unforgettable occasion. As the members of the congregation slowly and sadly filed out of the Abbey, following the minute's silence that had been observed

MOURNING ALL OVER THE WORLD
Crowds in Whitehall openly weep as Princess Diana's funeral procession passes by on its way to Westminster Abbey. It was, recalled one eyewitness, 'as though all of these people had lost someone incredibly dear to them'. The capital was at a complete standstill. Over a million people lined the route of the funeral cortege to the Abbey and along its final journey to the Spencer family home in Northamptonshire where the Princess was to be buried. In London, many had camped out along the route to be sure of their place. Around the world, a staggering 2.5 billion people – more than a third of the entire global population – were estimated to have watched the funeral live on television.

A SAD DAY AT WESTMINSTER ABBEY
The chief mourners behind Diana's coffin were, from left to right, the Prince of Wales, Prince Harry, Earl Spencer, Prince William and Prince Philip. Here, they stand to attention as the coffin-bearers turn to carry the Princess into the Abbey. Piers Morgan, who watched the funeral on television, noted in his diary: 'There were so many poignant moments, most notably those poor boys having to march down the Mall behind their dead mother ... I don't know how they handled it.' During the service, Elton John (above) sang a rewritten version of 'Candle in the Wind' re-titled 'Goodbye England's Rose'. It became the fastest-selling single of all time, with the proceeds going to the Diana, Princess of Wales, Memorial Fund.

across the nation, the events of the day as a whole and what Earl Spencer had said was on everyone's minds. Piers Morgan, one of the tabloid editors barred from the service, had arrived home hot from the *Daily Mirror* newsroom to host a lunch party. 'As I walked through the door', he wrote, 'the tears came again and I just sat crying in a chair, physically and emotionally exhausted, as everyone looked on in bemusement.' He continued: 'I have never reacted to any story like this, but then there has never been anyone in my professional life like Diana – and I guess part of my distress is also to do with the fact that there never will be again.' Millions would have agreed with his sentiments. For many, the dead Princess was simply irreplaceable.

What actually caused the crash was disputed for years. Repeated French and British criminal investigations found that Henri Paul, Al Fayed's chief of security at the Paris Ritz Hotel, was to blame for the accident – that he had been drinking before driving the car and speeding through the tunnel. Others – chief among them Mohammed Al Fayed, Dodi's grieving father – refused to accept the findings. Al Fayed claimed repeatedly that the couple had been murdered. They were, he insisted, the victims of a conspiracy masterminded by leading members of the British establishment. Despite all the evidence to the contrary, he stuck to his guns.

It took more than a decade for an inquest into the Princess's death to be held. By a majority verdict, the inquest jury found that the couple had been killed as a result of Henri Paul's drunken driving, although the activities of the paparazzi had also contributed to their deaths. It finally seemed clear that it had been a tragic accident, nothing more and nothing less.

DEVOLVING POWER

Traditionalists taken aback by the naked display of emotion that marked Diana's death were equally nonplussed by what seemed to be happening to the United Kingdom as a whole. True, the nation appeared to be prospering. By the turn of the millennium Gordon Brown, backed by a huge budget surplus, was claiming to be presiding over a new golden age. The bad old days of boom followed by bust, he asserted, had gone forever.

But not all change was seen as being for the best. Closer links with the European Union worried many, increased immigration into the UK bothered others. To some, the political fabric that held the United Kingdom together seemed in danger of being politically weakened. A few feared its outright disintegration.

CATHOLIC AND PROTESTANT
Murals on walls in Belfast bear witness to the Catholic community's opposition to the Orange Order marches, the all-too-visible public expression of extreme Ulster Protestantism. Though John Major had managed to get Nationalists and Unionists around the negotiating table, his efforts ended in stalemate. Tony Blair was determined to succeed where Major had failed. Eventually, a deal was struck. Northern Ireland, it was agreed, would be part of the UK for as long as the majority there wished it to remain so. Extremists on both sides would decommission their arms and there would be a new power-sharing executive. Peace, at long last, seemed a practical possibility in Northern Ireland.

THE BOMBERS' LAST THROW
Ulster's new Chief Minister, the Unionist David Trimble (third from left), and a delegation from the Northern Ireland Assembly survey the damage in the centre of Omagh, where a massive car bomb exploded a few months after the signing of the Good Friday Agreement. The horrific attack, the work of a renegade IRA splinter group, was intended to bring an end to the peace that had settled on the troubled province. Twenty-nine people were killed and 200 injured.

The Good Friday Agreement

Tony Blair had come to power determined to break the stalemate in Northern Ireland and bring peace to the battered province. With the active encouragement of US President Bill Clinton, the peace process was resurrected. Mo Mowlam, Blair's pugnacious Secretary of State for Northern Ireland, somehow managed to get Loyalists, Sinn Fein and government representatives from Dublin as well as London sitting together around the negotiating table. It was the first time that all sides had met together officially since 1921.

Progress was painfully slow at first. IRA outrages and Loyalist reprisals continued. Eventually, on Good Friday, 10 April, 1998, the representatives of the various parties reached agreement. 'It is time for the cycle of violence to be broken', Sinn Fein leader Gerry Adams told the Nationalists, going on to declare: 'We are prepared to break it.'

As the goal of a power-sharing Northern Ireland executive drew closer, Tony Blair arrived in Belfast to preside over the final stage of the negotiations. 'Now is not the time for soundbites', he told reporters, then proceeded to give them one, saying 'I can feel the hand of history upon my shoulders'. Soundbite or not, he was right. It was indeed a great historical moment as the centuries of violence that had scarred Irish history seemed at last to be coming to an end. In a referendum on the terms of the settlement, the people of Northern Ireland endorsed the agreement by a massive 71 per cent of those who voted.

Devolution for Scotland and Wales

Northern Ireland was not the only part of Britain to undergo constitutional reform. Almost as soon as New Labour took office, the question of a devolved parliament for Scotland appeared high on its agenda. On 11 September, 1997, the matter was put before the Scottish people in a referendum. Just over 60 per cent turned out to vote and the result was unequivocal: three-quarters of those who voted were in favour of a Scottish parliament. Slightly fewer agreed that it should have tax-raising powers.

In 1999, after a gap of three centuries, Scotland got back its Parliament. It was elected by proportional representation. The new Scottish executive had authority over education, health, welfare, local government, transport and housing. Labour politician Donald Dewer became the nation's First Minister, leading a Labour–Liberal Democrat coalition. The Scottish National Party, the Greens and Independents provided the opposition. The Conservatives failed to win a seat.

Wales, too, got its own Assembly, though there was less enthusiasm here for devolution than in Scotland. In the Welsh referendum the turnout was low and the devolutionists won just over 50 per cent of the vote. The 60-member Welsh Assembly had less power than its Scottish equivalent. Ron Davies, the Secretary of State for Wales, was considered its likely first leader until, just weeks after joining the Cabinet, he resigned after being robbed at knifepoint in what he himself termed 'a moment of madness' at dead of night on Clapham Common. Exactly what he was doing there – the Common was a well-known homosexual haunt – or why he felt it necessary to resign he never said. New Labour's Millbank machine ensured that Alun Michael, Blair's preferred candidate, became First Minister in his place. Rhodri Morgan, the grass-roots favourite, was simply passed over.

The Blair ascendancy

Blair also turned his attention to the House of Lords. Many agreed with him that it needed reforming, in particular to lessen dependence on the hereditary principle. After months of negotiation between peers and government, a compromise was reached. All save 92 of the 650 or so hereditary peers were removed from the Upper House. The lucky 92 were to be elected by the peers themselves. Then there was the Human Rights Act. This handed massive powers to the judges, who were charged with interpreting British legislation according to the terms of the European Convention. Parliament lost some degree of sovereignty as a result.

Davies's resignation proved to be little more than a blip as far as Blair and his administration were concerned. Peter Mandelson's was more serious, but the government managed to weather the storm unscathed. Nothing seemed to tarnish its popularity. In part this was due to the continued divisions and back-biting among the Conservatives. After Major's resignation, the leadership was won by William Hague, but though he was an able parliamentarian, when up against Blair he struggled to make his presence felt. 'The guy's a golf ball', scoffed Alan Clark, back in the Commons as MP for Kensington and Chelsea. When Hague attended the Notting Hill Carnival wearing a baseball cap, rather than making him look like he possessed the popular touch, the image simply made people laugh.

Blair sailed on triumphantly, becoming more presidential in his manner by the day. New Labour, it was obvious, was here to stay. As Britain approached the millennium, there seemed no good reason why Blair and his party should not go on governing and modernising well into the next century.

HISTORIC DAY FOR SCOTLAND
Scotland's newly appointed First Minister Donald Dewar, with David Steel, the former Liberal leader, makes his way into the first official session of the Scottish Assembly in July 1999. Devolution for both Scotland and Wales had long been a Labour Party promise that Tony Blair was determined to fulfil. Almost as soon as Labour won the 1997 general election, a referendum was held in Scotland to decide the nation's future. Some 60 per cent of Scots voted, of whom 74 per cent voted for a Scottish Parliament; 63.5 per cent demanded that such a Parliament have its own tax-raising powers. Slightly later, a similar referendum was held in Wales. Though the majority in favour of devolution was much smaller, Blair decided that a Welsh Assembly should be set up as well.

A THOUSAND
YEARS ENDS

As the end of the century drew ever nearer, many people pondered the best way of marking the dawn of the new millennium. Pedants argued that, strictly speaking, the correct night to celebrate was 31 December, 2000. Prominent among them was John Howard, Australia's prime minister, who was promptly dubbed 'party pooper of the century' by his fellow Aussies. The vast majority had no doubt that the right night to party was 31 December, 1999.

THE WOBBLY BRIDGE Linking Bankside and the City, London's Millennium Bridge opened on 10 June, 2000. Three days later it was closed due to what engineers technically termed 'synchronous lateral excitation' – in other words, it wobbled. It reopened, wobble-free, in 2002.

MILLENNIUM BUILDINGS

In Britain, work on planning the celebrations to mark the turn of the millennium had begun as early as 1994, when John Major put Michael Heseltine in charge of the newly established Millennium Commission. It chose the Greenwich peninsula in east London, an area in desperate need of regeneration, to be centre stage as the site of a vast Millennium Dome; Birmingham and Derby were the unsuccessful candidates. The Dome was to house exhibitions, displays and performances that would be the focus of the country's gigantic millennium celebrations. The estimated cost was £580 million. The London Eye, the largest Ferris wheel in the world at the time of its construction, and the Millennium footbridge over the Thames were also to be built as part of the overall plans to mark the momentous occasion in the capital.

In terms of national celebrations, the Dome had plenty of precedents. The Festival of Britain in 1951, the British Empire Exhibition held in Wembley in 1924 and the Great Exhibition of 1851 had all been hugely successful events that captured the spirit of their times. Tony Blair wanted the celebrations staged on his watch to be just as memorable. At a press conference called to launch the project in February 1998, he explained how, after debating long and hard as to whether to continue with the project, the Cabinet had come down in favour of building the Dome. 'I want today's children', he said, 'to take from it an experience so powerful and memories so strong that it gives them that abiding sense of purpose and unity that stays with them for the rest of their lives.'

MARKING THE MILLENNIUM
Throughout the UK, major building projects got underway during the countdown to the Millennium. The Gateshead Millennium Bridge, a new link across the River Tyne between Gateshead and Newcastle (top right), was the world's first tilting bridge. The design was chosen by a public vote in an architectural competition. In Cardiff, the Millennium Stadium (bottom left) was built to provide the national rugby team with a new home fit for the 21st century, replacing the ageing Arms Park. It cost £121 million to build – compared to the Dome, many thought it was extremely good value – and was completed on schedule in time for Wales to host the 1999 Rugby World Cup. One of its most remarkable features was a fully retractable roof. Most of the building projects were welcomed. The Dome (bottom right) was the exception. From the start, voices argued against it because of cost and, though it opened on schedule, its life as an exhibition centre was dogged by criticism and financial problems. Eventually, it was sold off to private enterprise.

AN EYE OVER LONDON

RAISING THE WHEEL

Passengers on the London Eye look down over the Thames to Big Ben, the Houses of Parliament and beyond from one of the 32 egg-shaped capsules (left). Each capsule can carry up to 25 passengers and the wheel revolves at the stately pace of 26cm (10in) per second, taking around half an hour to complete a full revolution. Construction was not without its problems. Sections of the wheel were floated up the Thames on barges and assembled flat on specially built piled platforms in the river. Once the wheel was complete, an elaborate jacking system was employed to hoist it into position. It was slowly raised in two stages; once the wheel had reached an angle of 65 degrees, the raising was halted for engineers to check it for stability before the final stage commenced. The process took several days. Most people marvelled, but as ever there were some who were not impressed. One eyewitness said: 'It looks like a giant bicycle wheel with spokes. I assume it works all right, but it looks highly dangerous to me. I'm not going on it!'

When Tony Blair opened the Millennium Wheel on 31 December, 1999, there was only one problem: it wasn't ready. It finally opened for business in March 2000. Despite the delay caused by technical teething problems, the Eye emerged as one of the Millennium's great successes, becoming a familiar part of London's riverside skyline. By 2007, 30 million people had taken a trip on it. Architect Sir Richard Rogers commented; 'The Eye has done for London what the Eiffel Tower did for Paris, which is to give it a symbol and to let people climb above the city and look back down on it. Not just specialists and rich people, but everybody. That's the beauty of it.'

The Prime Minister had lofty ideals about the purpose of the celebrations and the Dome. 'The millennium', he said, 'is an important time for us all to reflect on our common past, the present we share, and the future we will help to shape. In this country, at this time, I believe we can stand proud as forward-looking people who are breaking down old-fashioned barriers, building a multiracial Britain that works, seizing new opportunities, creating new products, building strong communities. I am confident that, in the next millennium as in this, the British people will be characterised by their ingenuity, their determination and their compassion.' They were fine words but some people began to wonder how such sentiments would translate into a meaningful exhibition.

Back in 1951, the Festival of Britain had had a clearly defined purpose. It was intended to be 'a tonic for the nation', to show that the country had faith in its future and was well on the way to recovering from the privations of the Second World War. The self-proclaimed aim of the British Empire Exhibition had been to 'strengthen the bonds that bind the Mother Country to her sister states and daughter nations', while the Great Exhibition was an unabashed

> 'The Millennium Dome was intended to be New Labour's Xanadu and Tony Blair its Kubla Khan.'
>
> Andrew Rawnsley, from *Servants of the People*

ANGEL OF THE NORTH

British artist Antony Gormley created this massive steel sculpture, aptly christened the Angel of the North, to stand on a hill on the southern appoach to the northeastern town of Gateshead. Unveiled in 1998 and standing on a site once occupied by a colliery, it was intended to be an eloquent tribute to the region's industrial heritage. Made from 208 tonnes of a special weather-resistant mix of copper and steel, the Angel stands 20 metres high and spans 54 metres in total, almost the same width as the wings of a Boeing 747 jumbo jet. The sculpture was erected at a cost of £800,000 and showed, according to the *Shropshire Star*, 'the soft southerners that there's more to the North East than brown ale, unemployment and football'.

ART POWER-HOUSE

Visitors to Tate Modern, created in 2000 out of what was once a power station on the South Bank of the Thames opposite St Paul's Cathedral, make their way through the huge display area of the Turbine Hall. The original building, designed by Sir Giles Gilbert Scott, was a strikingly original piece of architecture in its own right; Swiss architects Jacques Herzog and Pierre de Merron won the job of adapting Scott's original design for its new purpose – to provide a worthy home for the national collection of international modern art. The two men succeeded brilliantly. The cavernous Turbine Hall became a dramatic entrance area and a display space for very large sculptural projects. The boiler house was converted to house the museum's galleries, set on three levels and running the entire length of the massive building.

celebration of the Industrial Revolution and the revolutionary changes that had come in its wake. Whether the Millennium Dome could live up to these inspiring precedents was far from clear. For some, Blair's comment that it should be 'exhilarating like Disney World and emotionally uplifting like a West End musical' did not inspire confidence. Peter Mandelson, who had been in charge of the project until his enforced resignation from Cabinet, at least put it more directly and succinctly. 'I want', he said, 'to knock their socks off.'

Building the Dome

Designed by architect Sir Richard Rogers and his team, the Dome was a controversial building right from the start. It was to be the largest structure of its kind in the world when construction work began in 1997. This involved first driving 8,000 piles into the ground to provide the necessary support for the foundations. Then 12 huges masts were erected to support the cable network that would give the Dome its characteristic shape. The structural job was completed in March 1998, after which came the installation of the roof, which consisted of 72 giant pieces of glass fibre coated in Teflon. Work on the service buildings inside the Dome's inner core had already begun that January. Exactly a year after the start of construction, the Prime Minister arrived in Greenwich to preside over the building's topping-out ceremony.

The big question now was what was to go inside it – and who would pay to go and see it. What emerged in the planning was to divide the interior into three distinct areas – 'Who We Are', 'What We Do' and 'Where We Live' – between them housing 14 zones. The first area featured zones on Body, Mind, Faith and the strangely titled Self-Portrait; the second focused on Work, Learning, Rest, Play, Talk, Money and Journey; the third consisted of Shared Ground, Living Island and Home Planet. At the centre was a performance area where, with the aid of an acrobatic cast of 160 and specially composed music by rock star Peter Gabriel, the Millennium Dome Show was to be performed on the night. Many were unhappy with the proposals. Chief among them was design guru Stephen Bayley, who resigned as the Dome's Creative Director following a major falling-out with Peter Mandelson. The Dome, he warned bluntly, 'could turn out to be crap', especially if Mandelson was allowed to continue 'running the project like a dictator'.

The planning team pressed ahead regardless, but what they failed to anticipate was that a shortfall in the take-up of tickets would cause financial problems. Sure enough, initial ticket sales, on which the grandly named New Millennium Experience Company was relying, turned out to be woefully below what had been confidently forecast. The company had to turn to the Millennium Commission for an emergency bail-out in order to survive. It was just the first rescue of many.

WANTED MAN
Protesters wearing masks of Augusto Pinochet and Margaret Thatcher demonstrate outside the magistrate's court where Pinochet was fighting an attempt to extradite him to Spain. The former President of Chile was wanted to stand trial for crimes committed during his tyrannical regime, including the torture and murder of political prisoners. He was arrested in London in October 1998 after coming to Britain for medical treatment. During the ensuing legal battle, which lasted for 15 months, Mrs Thatcher was a prominent voice calling for his release; the tea cups and saucers are a reference to them taking tea together on Pinochet's visits to London. Pinochet was released in March 2000 on medical grounds and returned home to a hero's welcome. He died in 2006, aged 91.

NEW LABOUR AT HOME

The Dome may not have been Blair's finest hour, but true to form his personal popularity remained undimmed. New Labour's conduct of home affairs in general was not proving particularly impressive, either. There was much talk of 'Blair's cronies' and of Downing Street's ever-increasing tendency to rely on spin-doctors and backstairs attempts to by-pass parliamentary debate and discussion. Peter Mandelson's return to the Cabinet – in October 1999 he replaced Mo Mowlam as Secretary of State for Northern Ireland – seemed to be a clear indication that spin was back in fashion, but he did bring his considerable powers of persuasion to the task of putting the Good Friday Agreement into practice.

'… the party of fox-hunting, Pinochet and hereditary peers – the uneatable, the unspeakable and the unelectable.'

Tony Blair, referring to the Conservatives at the Labour Party conference, 1999

Meanwhile, hundreds of hours of parliamentary time were being devoted to the rights and wrongs of fox-hunting, with the Prime Minister sitting uncomfortably on the fence between on the one hand those country-dwellers who were resolutely opposed to a ban and on the other the left-wingers on his backbenches who were equally determined to impose one. In the end, Blair came down in favour of taking some form of legislative action. And at the party conference in Bournemouth in 1999, he was not averse to using the issue to gain a cheer from the ranks as he promised to sweep away the 'forces of Conservatism'.

TALLY-HO
A lone protester holds up an anti-hunting newspaper advertisement as demonstrators arrive in Hyde Park to take part in a pro-hunting rally (top left). Veteran anti-hunting protester Frank Fitch (bottom) poses with a rescued fox during an anti-hunting demonstration at Maldon in Essex. The banning of fox-hunting came high on the list of New Labour priorities. As the prospect of legislation loomed, hunt supporters banded together in the Countryside Alliance to defend the right to hunt. The Alliance's first big rally, held in Hyde Park shortly after the 1997 General Election, drew a 120,000 crowd. Opposing them, the League Against Cruel Sports and the Hunt Saboteurs Association were just as determined to see a ban enforced.

The Brown factor
By this time, however, Blair, who had come to some form of concordat with Gordon Brown which gave the Chancellor the final say in many domestic policy matters, was seemingly becoming less interested in affairs on the home front. He had tried, but failed, to get Brown to take a serious look at the ever-increasing problems of adequately funding the welfare state. The pensions expert Frank Field, whom Blair had put in charge of social security reform with the brief to 'think the unthinkable', found himself sidelined; Field resigned when told that he would have to move sideways in the 1998 Cabinet reshuffle. Nor would Brown countenance any move to commit Britain to abandoning the pound in favour of the Euro. The 'five economic tests' that he and his Treasury civil servants had devised – and insisted must be met before entry to the new European currency could be considered – effectively blocked the Prime Minister's pro-Euro policy.

It was largely froth and very little substance. Characteristic of the times was the great dot-com boom, triggered by venture capitalists pouring start-up funds into what, in many cases, were to prove disastrous e-commerce investments. When the dot.com bubble burst, there were many casualties. The UK-based on-line fashion retailer Boo.com was the most notorious of the failures. Opening for business on the Web in autumn 1999, it burned through $135 million of investment capital in just 18 months before collapsing into administration. No one got any money back.

DERBY DAY

SPORT OF KINGS AND COMMONERS
As always, race goers thronged to Epsom for Derby Day in June 1997; the man with the fat cigar is a tipster checking the form. It was the 218th meeting of Britain's top flat-racing classic. The outsider Benny the Dip, with jockey Willie Ryan in the saddle, won the race, beating Silver Patriarch ridden by Pat Eddery in one of the closest Derby finishes of all time; Entrepreneur, the pre-race favourite, came fourth.

Racing maintained its traditional popularity during the 1990s, with more than 6 million people attending race meetings annually across the land. Flat and National Hunt racing were equally popular. In 1996 Cheltenham, voted race-course of the year four times in succession, set a new record for daily attendance with 58,500 spectators at the course to watch that year's Cheltenham Gold Cup.

TEAM SPORTS AND THEIR FANS

To judge by the numbers of fans, football was the undisputed king of spectator sports by the end of the millennium. In 1996 it was England's turn to host the European Championship and fans came in their thousands to cheer on their national teams. England and Scotland had both qualified for the tournament; the Scots were knocked out in the first round, while England lost on penalties to Germany – the eventual winners – in the semi-finals. Though fewer in number, rugby supporters were just as loyal. In 1999, in addition to the annual Six Nations tournament, they had the Rugby World Cup to savour. England, Wales and Scotland all lost their respective quarter-final matches; the eventual winners were Australia. The Aussies swept all before them in cricket, too. At the end of the decade, it looked as though they might keep the Ashes forever.

FANATICAL FANS
Regardless of the sport, fans were always ready to support their national teams. These face-painted Scottish rugby supporters (left) are cheering on the home side during the 1991 Rugby World Cup play-off between Scotland and New Zealand; the All Blacks won by 13 points to six. Football fans were even more fanatical; the pictures here show (clockwise from top left) Spanish, Dutch, German and Turkish supporters, gaily face-painted and costumed to confirm their national identities before the start of various key matches in soccer's 1996 European Championship, hosted by England. It was not all smiles, however; ongoing football hooliganism worried and outraged many followers of the sport.

ON TOP OF THE WORLD
Manchester United crowned a decade of achievement with victory in the 1999 European Cup. They defeated Bayern Munich 2-1 in the final, held in Barcelona; here (above), the team savour the moment. It was the first time they had won the European Cup since 1968, when they became the second British team to lift the ultimate club trophy. The first was Celtic, who had won the previous year. In 1999 United had already won the Double – the League Championship and FA Cup – for the third time since 1994. Soon after their triumph in Spain United's Scottish manager, Alex Ferguson, was knighted for services to football.

United played most of the game against Munich trailing by a goal to nil, but they scored two stunning goals in injury time to clinch victory from the jaws of defeat. Sheringham and Solksjaer were their last-minute goal-scorers. The turnaround was so unexpected that when UEFA President Lennart Johansson left his seat in the stands to prepare for the presentation, the trophy was already decorated with Bayern Munich ribbons. Johansson was nonplussed when he made it onto the pitch after the final whistle: 'I can't believe it', he said. 'The winners are crying and the losers are dancing.' The ultimate proof that two minutes can be a long time in football.

'I can't believe it. I can't believe it. Football. Bloody hell.'

Alex Ferguson after Manchester United snatched a surprise victory in the 1999 European Cup Final

INTERNATIONAL RUGBY

Rugby Union was revolutionised in 1995, when the International Rugby Board made the sport fully professional. The amateur–professional divide had been the major distinction between rugby union and rubgy league since the 19th century, when the rules of the game were established. Since then the two games had diverged, but the change nonetheless opened up the union game to league players who would previously have been barred for being professionals. The aim behind the change was to improve the union game, but England was slow to reap benefits. In 1998, during the so-called 'tour from Hell', they were hammered 76-0 by Australia, the worst defeat in English rugby history.

Fans flocked to see the best international teams battle it out in the new Rugby World Cup. The first tournament was played in 1987 in Australia and New Zealand. Four years later England hosted the second competition. Despite the home team's best efforts – legendary captain Will Carling (top) is seen brilliantly side-stepping two Australian defenders – they lost to the Wallabies, who went on to win the tournament.

In 1999, World Cup action moved to Wales, where the finalists battled it out in the country's brand-new Millennium Stadium. The Welsh got off to a good start, beating Argentina by 23 points to 18; Welsh fly-half Neil Jenkins is seen here taking a penalty kick (right). In the quarter-finals they came up against Australia, who won by 24 points to nine. The Wallabies were playing brilliant rugby and so were the French, who knocked out pre-tournament favourites New Zealand. When Australia and France met in the final, it was the Wallabies who triumphed, becoming the first team to win the trophy twice.

PEACE AND WAR

Bolstered by his success in brokering a peace settlement in Northern Ireland, Tony Blair devoted more and more of his time to making a mark on the international stage. Having established cordial relations with President Clinton, in December 1998 he ordered RAF bombers to join with the US Air Force in bombing targets in Iraq. The object of the operation, which lasted for four days, was to punish Saddam Hussein for his obstruction of the work of the UN weapons inspectors. The RAF went into action again in war-torn Yugoslavia, when British and US jets attacked targets in Kosovo and then the rest of Serbia in an effort to bring an end to the campaign of so-called ethnic cleansing that the Serbs were carrying out against the Muslim inhabitants of the region.

FOREIGN INTERESTS

Foreign Secretary Robin Cook and Tony Blair chat with US President Bill Clinton. Cook promised to pursue a new ethical foreign policy, but he soon found himself under fire. Blair supported Clinton when the latter authorised the bombing of a supposed terrorist base in Afghanistan and also what was claimed to be a chemical weapons plant in Sudan – it turned out to be a veterinary pharmaceuticals factory. Blair and Clinton then authorised the use of cruise missiles to bomb 250 targets in Iraq. Many doubted whether the bombing was effective. Cynics suspected that Clinton ordered the action to distract from his political troubles at home. Robin Cook resigned from the government in 2003 over the invasion of Iraq. He died in 2005.

CONFLICT IN SERBIA

Tony Blair led the way in pressing for NATO action against Serbia to put an end to the ethnic cleansing that Serb forces were carrying out in the province of Kosovo. Accordingly, British and American jets were sent into the attack – first in Kosovo and then against Serbia itself. Air power on its own did not prove to be enough to force the Serbs to back down; it was only when Russia and the USA threatened military intervention on the ground that Serbia withdrew its troops from war-torn Kosovo. Tony Blair justified the action as an act of liberation, but it did not go unchallenged. Here, Serbs in London protest against the decision to send the RAF into action against their homeland.

SWEET TASTE OF SUCCESS
A Kosovan Albanian raises Tony Blair's arm in the air during the latter's whistle-stop visit to Pristina in July 1999. It was the Prime Minister's first visit to the region following the conclusion of the NATO bombing campaign against the Serbs. Though his willingness to take Britain into war in the Balkans had divided opinion at home, there was no doubting the enthusiasm with which he was received in Kosovo. The liberated Kosovans hailed him as their saviour, chanting his name over and over. The jubilant Prime Minister told them that Britain had 'fought in this conflict for a cause and that cause was justice'.

FOND FAREWELL
Kosovan children say goodbye to their British protectors as NATO forces pull out of Brazda Camp, their peacekeeping mission in the area over. Tony Blair had been horrified by the human suffering the Serbs had caused. Visiting a refugee camp, he exclaimed angrily: 'This is obscene. It's criminal … How can anyone think we shouldn't intervene.' Back in London, he ordered that 50,000 troops, the bulk of the available army, should be made ready to invade Kosovo. Fortunately for him and the British army, the Serbs backed down under the threat of armed intervention before Blair's resolution could be put to the test.

The action was a failure. The Serbs rallied behind their leaders and, rather than stopping, ethnic cleansing actually intensified. Blair urged Clinton to send troops into action on the ground; he himself ordered plans to be prepared to send 50,000 British soldiers into Kosovo. Luckily, at the last minute the Serbs buckled under the pressure. Right, Blair proclaimed, had triumphed. 'We fought in this conflict for a cause', he told a crowd of cheering Kosovans on a lightning visit to the war zone, 'and that cause was justice.'

The consequences were awesome. The bombing of Iraq, the Kosovo affair and a successful intervention in Sierra Leone to restore the moderate government that had been overthrown in a *coup d'état*, combined to convince Blair that he was a natural war leader, prepared to take gambles and get them right. This belief was to colour his later actions in his premiership. For now, though, this was in the future. For the present – at home, at least – things seemed stable, secure, prosperous and safe. What the new millennium would bring was a matter of speculation.

MILLENNIUM EVE

The Dome opened on 31 December, 1999, with a New Millennium show for the great and the good. The Queen, the Duke of Edinburgh, the Prime Minister and his wife were among those who went to Greenwich to party. It was doomed from the start. Piers Morgan turned down his invitation, writing in his diary: 'I couldn't think of anything worse in the entire world than spending the dawn of the next 1,000 years with a bunch of politicians.' He later went on to note how 'all the editors who did make the effort got left for hours at Stratford station with a plastic cup of warm wine', from which he drew the conclusion: 'That will be the end of the Dome then.'

Morgan was right. Most of the newspapers lost little time in savaging the Dome and its exhibition, although a few begged to differ. For the writer Adam Nicolson, 'the Dome was a catalogue of marvels, a cabinet of rarities, a circus of marvels … a kaleidoscope of the very best that we could do.' But Nicolson was in a distinct minority. The Dome, the majority agreed, was a flop – rather like the Y2K bug, which the pessimists had warned was going to crash computers and cripple networks around the world, but in the event never materialised.

Queues for the most popular Dome zones were catastrophically long, while most of them were condemned as lacking any hard content. The Journey zone, featuring the history and development of transport, was one of the few singled

'I hate to join the chortling ranks of Dome rubbishers in the right-wing press, but alas I have to admit the Dome is a lemon.'

Polly Toynbee, *The Guardian*, January 2000

out for praise. By the time the Dome closed on 31 December, 2000, just over 6 million visitors had paid to explore it, which was only half the number that the New Millennium Experience Company had counted on.

Other features of Britain's Millennium celebrations fared rather better. Even if last-minute safety checks on the London Eye meant that, on the night, it could turn but not carry passengers, the big wheel became a popular attraction when it finally opened for business in March. The Tate Modern art gallery, housed in a brilliantly converted power station on the south bank of the Thames, was hailed as an architectural triumph. So, too, was Norman Foster's redesigning of the newly glass-topped British Museum. In Cardiff, the Millennium Stadium wowed the crowds, while up in the northeast the Gateshead Millenium Bridge and a towering new sculpture – 'The Angel of the North' – won many admirers. British artists, too, were in the ascendant. Like them or loathe them, the controversial works of Damien Hirst and Tracey Emin, the two leading figures in the BritArt movement, were noted for their challenging originality.

FUN FAIR ON THE MALL
In London, thousands packed into a special Millennium Eve fun fair set up on Pall Mall at the behest of a benevolent government. Official celebrations were put on up and down the country, but most people preferred to celebrate in their own way. Magazine writer Nick Setchfield recalled nearly a decade later how he spent the crucial moments with friends at the top of a hill near Bath: 'We swigged champagne from plastic cups, Mark pledging to down champers every day of his life from now on. Viv gave me my first kiss of the next thousand years … Fireworks erupted across the horizon, gunpowder blossomed in the rain. All my cynicism had been coughed up, or sneezed away … This was good.'

HAPPY NEW YEAR ... HAPPY NEW CENTURY ... HAPPY NEW MILLENNIUM Tony and Cherie Blair sing 'Auld Lang Syne' with enthusiasm as midnight strikes on New Year's Eve, 1999, at the party held in the Millennium Dome. The Queen looks less-than-amused and who could blame her, having done her duty as ever and turned out to sit through a long and less-than-spectacular show. The Dome occasion, many felt, was something of an anticlimax. Outside, meanwhile, London's skies were lit up by a magnificent firework display (right).

Parties across Britain

On the night, millions of people turned out nationwide to join in one great party. A chain of 1,400 beacons were lit across the country, starting off in the islands of Scotland and progressing southwards. London, Edinburgh, Cardiff and Belfast all had giant beacons – the capital's, lit by the Queen herself, was the world's biggest. Other highlights included a hair-raising 300-metre high-wire walk slung between two church spires in Coventry, a string quartet suspended over the crowds in Newcastle upon Tyne, a bridge of laser light across the River Mersey in Liverpool and a Millennium time-tunnel under the Lagan Weir in Belfast.

In London, an estimated 4 million people partied in the streets. Many of them congregated in Trafalgar Square and in the royal parks. Others gathered on the banks and bridges of the Thames, waiting for the midnight fireworks display, which would climax, it was promised, with the river appearing to be set alight. Science fiction writer Geoff Ryman recollected that it seemed as if 'all of London had been drinking a toast all along the river'. Other cities were not to be outdone, especially in Scotland, the home of the New Year's Eve party. According to the *Edinburgh Evening News*, the Scottish capital's Millennium Hogmanay 'exceeded all expectation' with almost 200,000 revellers packing the historic city centre, 'cheering, clasping and kissing each other to welcome in the New Year in Scotland's biggest street party'. Glasgow city centre 'exploded with a cacophony of cheers, kisses and even a few tears' as 100,000 people partied and partied.

Not everyone got into the swing of the celebrations. Scriptwriter Russell T Davies, the brains behind *Doctor Who*, recalled a decade later that, on the night, he had 'a stinking cold. My ears and head were stuffed full, like I was trapped inside a sleeping bag. So we went to my old mate Alex's for dinner, visited the neighbours, fireworks went off in the rain ... all I wanted to do was to go home.' And that was it. The end of the millennium and the beginning of a new century.

INDEX

Page numbers in *italic* refer to the captions.

PICTURE ACKNOWLEDGEMENTS

Abbreviations: t = top; m = middle; b = bottom; r = right; c = centre; l = left
All images in this book are courtesy of Getty Images, including the following which have additional attributions:

Front cover, 30, 31, 40, 41, 45, 46, 47, 52, 53b, 59, 67, 84, 86, 87b, 89, 90, 91, 100, 106, 107, 112, 113, 117l, 117r, 118tr, 119t, 121, 122, 123, 124r, 125, 128, 129, 130, 131, 135, 138, 141, 142, 149b, 150, 157b: Agence France Presse
Back cover, 12-13, 35t, 37, 50, 96, 98, 101, 103, 105, 157t: Tom Stoddart Archive
2, 17, 42, 48, 60, 62, 82, 108, 120: Tim Graham Photo Library

4, 6-7, 8-9, 10-11, 14, 18, 19, 25, 54, 55, 56-57, 64, 68, 70-71, 74, 75, 76, 77, 79, 87t, 102, 104, 144, 145, 151, 154: Steve Eason
20, 93, 118tl: Terry O'Neill
23, 33, 34, 35b, 36, 39, 69, 78, 88, 92, 94: Peter Macdiarmid
24, 51r, 53t, 81: Time & Life Pictures
26: John Lamb
27: Jim Dyson
28: Science & Society Picture Library
51l: Conservative Party Archives
72: Michael Birt

95: Michael Putland
110: Redferns/ Mick Hutson
111, 114, 115, 116, 117m, 119b: Dave Benett
118b: WireImage
124l, 126, 156: Anwar Hussein
127: Princess Diana Archive
136: Jonathan Elderfield
137: Michael Porro
139: Carlos Lopez-Barillas
147tr, 147b: Bongarts
152t: David Brauchli
152b: Ami Vitale

LOOKING BACK AT BRITAIN
TOWARDS A NEW MILLENNIUM – 1990s
Published in 2011 in the United Kingdom by
Vivat Direct Limited (t/a Reader's Digest) in association
with Getty Images and Endeavour London Limited

Vivat Direct Limited
(t/a Reader's Digest)
157 Edgware Road
London W2 2HR

Endeavour London Limited
21–31 Woodfield Road
London W9 2BA
info@endeavourlondon.com

Copyright © 2011 Vivat Direct Limited

Colour origination by Chroma Graphics Ltd, Singapore
Printed and bound in Europe by Arvato Iberia, Portugal

For Endeavour
Publisher: Charles Merullo
Designer: Tea Aganovic
Picture editors: Jennifer Jeffrey, Franziska Payer Crockett
Production: Mary Osborne

For Vivat Direct
Editorial director: Julian Browne
Art director: Anne-Marie Bulat
Project editor: Christine Noble
Art editor: Conorde Clarke
Indexer: Marie Lorimer
Proofreader: Ron Pankhurst
Pre-press technical manager: Dean Russcll
Product production manager: Claudette Bramble
Production controller: Sandra Fuller

Written by
Jeremy Harwood

We are committed both to the quality of our products
and the service we provide to our customers.
We value your comments, so please do contact us on
08705 113366 or via our website at
www.readersdigest.co.uk

If you have any comments or suggestions about
the content of our books, email us at
gbeditorial@readersdigest.co.uk

CONCEPT CODE: UK 0154/L/S
BOOK CODF: 638-015 UP0000-1
ISBN: 978 0 276 44403 6